Violence against Children

This volume is published as part of a long-standing cooperative program between Harvard University Press and the Commonwealth Fund, a philanthropic foundation, to encourage the publication of significant scholarly books in medicine and health.

David G. Gil

Violence against Children

Physical Child Abuse in the United States

Harvard University Press
Cambridge, Massachusetts, and London, England

A Commonwealth Fund Book

Library of Congress Catalog Card Number 77-130809
ISBN 0-674-93900-0
Printed in the United States of America
10   9

to my parents

Preface

to the Paperback Edition

The publication of *Violence against Children* as a paperback, three years after its initial publication, offers an opportunity to note briefly several developments reflecting a growing awareness of the rights of children, developments which may have been facilitated by the findings and recommendations presented in this book.

One of the more important insights gained through the nation-wide studies of child abuse reported in this volume was that violence against children is not a rare occurrence, but may be endemic in our society because of a child rearing philosophy which sanctions, and even encourages, the use of physical force in disciplining children. Furthermore, it became clear that abuse of children committed or tolerated by society as a whole, by permitting millions of children to grow up under conditions of severe deprivation, was a much more serious social problem than abusive acts toward children committed by individual caretakers. Not surprisingly, it was also learned that while child abuse is known to occur among all groups in the population, children living in deprived circumstances were, for a variety of reasons, more likely than other children to be subjected to abusive acts by their care-takers. Finally, the study revealed that children are being abused physically and emotionally not only in their own homes, but also in the public domain, in schools, and in other child care settings, especially those schools and institutions that serve children from economically depressed neighborhoods. The dynamics of child abuse were thus found to be deeply rooted in the fabric of our culture. Consequently, the widespread notion that this destructive phenomenon was primarily a symptom of individual psycho-pathology appeared to be too narrow an interpretation of the wide spectrum of child abuse.

In view of these findings, I suggested several logical approaches toward the reduction and eventual prevention of all violence against the young in our society. We must attack this violence at its sources by changing our prevailing child rearing philosophy and practice. We must reject the use of physical force in disciplining children and we must eliminate poverty which now keeps millions of children from realizing their human potential.

One obvious setting in which to initiate shifts in child rearing philosophy and practices is the public domain, and more specifically, schools and child care settings outside the child's own family. During the past three years many concerned parents, lawyers, human services professionals, journalists, and civil rights groups all over the United States engaged in attempts to protect the rights of children to dignity and to bodily integrity in schools and in other public settings. These attempts involved court suits and lobbying for appropriate protective state and federal legislation. Results of these efforts are so far limited which is not surprising in view of the deep-seated traditions which shape prevailing child rearing practices, and which need to be overcome if fundamental changes are to be widely accepted. Yet, some encouraging progress has taken place. Massachusetts last year followed New Jersey's earlier example and enacted sweeping legislation prohibiting all forms of corporal punishment in its schools and correctional facilities, after defeating similar legislation for two years in a row, mainly because of objections from teachers and school principals. Bills modeled after the new Massachusetts law are now being promoted in several states. Numerous law suits now in progress in the federal courts argue that the constitutional rights of children as persons are infringed on several counts whenever they are subjected to corporal punishment in schools or other public facilities. One such case, which originated in Dallas, Texas, reached the U.S. Supreme Court, but was not granted a hearing. The constitutional questions concerning corporal punishment remain thus unresolved for the time being, although the Supreme Court has ruled in recent years that children are persons in the sense of the Constitution and are hence entitled to equal protection of their civil rights, and to due process.

In May 1972, the American Civil Liberties Union, which had become interested in the rights of children as a non-vocal and unrepresented segment of the population, sponsored a nation-wide conference in order to integrate ongoing, local efforts against corporal punishment in the schools into a national movement. The major result of this conference was the formation of the National Committee To Abolish Corporal Punishment In The Schools and a national clearing house for the exchange of legal briefs and other materials pertaining to the protection of children's rights in courts and before legislatures. At about the same time that the National Committee To Abolish Corporal Punishment was organized in the United States, an international, interdisciplinary association for the study and prevention of filicide was founded with headquarters in Buenos Aires, Argentina. This association held its first international congress in the summer of 1973 in Paris, France.

While there has been some progress over the past three years toward a lower level of violence against children in our schools, and a determined advocacy movement seems to be evolving to promote and protect the human and civil rights of children, no noteworthy progress is as yet discernable concerning the elimination of poverty —an even more salient aspect of the prevention of child abuse.

Perhaps we may even be regressing on that score, as we seem not even ready to recognize the multiple linkages between social and economic deprivation and violence against children.

One other controversial policy recommended in this book as a potential means for reducing the incidence of child abuse on the part of individual perpetrators is the repeal of laws interferring with the free availability of contraceptive information and devices, as well as the right of women to obtain medical abortions. During the last three years marked progress has taken place on these issues, including decisions of the U.S. Supreme Court upholding a broad scope of rights concerning contraception and abortions. There is by now reliable evidence of a decline in the birthrate due in part to ready availability of contraception and abortions. No doubt, this means fewer unwanted children, and hence, fewer candidates for infanticide, battering of babies, and other forms of individual child abuse.

It may now be of interest to examine whether the developments sketched here do to some extent reflect the findings and interpretations presented in *Violence against Children* on the basis of nationwide studies, and whether professional and public attitudes toward this phenomenon have been influenced in the meantime by these findings and interpretations. While these developments and attitudes over recent years seem to suggest a growing awareness of the multi-dimensional nature of child abuse, the view that violence against children results mainly from psychological disorders of perpetrators appears nevertheless to be dominant. Hence, existing and proposed policies and programs for the detection, treatment, and prevention of child abuse continue to be clinically oriented and tend to disregard in their conception and design the roots of this phenomenon in the fabric of society and in prevailing institutional arrangements. Such programs may of course alleviate the suffering of victims of abuse, and are thus important community resources. Yet, in spite of their claims and expectations, these policies and programs do not affect the sources and dynamics of present and future child abuse, and viewing them as preventative measures is therefore merely an illusion.

Perhaps the most recent illustration of the prevailing professional and public attitudes concerning child abuse at the time of this writing is Senate Bill 1191, which Senator Walter F. Mondale of Minnesota with thirteen other senators as co-sponsors, introduced in the U.S. Senate on March 13, 1973. This bill, the "Child Abuse Prevention Act of 1973," is based on the conventional, clinical model and would establish federal support for clinically oriented treatment services in communities throughout the country. No doubt, if enacted, the bill would aid some children and families, but in spite of the claims implicit in its title, would not prevent, nor even reduce significantly, the overall incidence of child abuse. As originally proposed, the bill did not define the concept of child abuse and included no provisions against corporal punishment in schools and child care settings, nor for the elimination of socially sanctioned forms of deprivation to which so many children are now exposed. Also, the bill did not spell out the rights to which children should be entitled, and thus, failed to establish criteria for identifying and preventing abusive incidents and conditions. As the author of *Violence against Children,* I was invited to testify on this bill before the U.S. Senate Subcommittee on Children and Youth. The testimony I presented on that occasion seems to highlight our current dilemmas concerning the persistence of violence against children in our society and is, therefore, included as Appendix F in this book.

D.G.G.
Lexington, Massachusetts
April 19, 1973

Preface

In recent decades interest in physical abuse of children on the part of professional groups, government agencies, and the general public has increased constantly in the United States.[1] This growing interest and the related, at times sensational, publicity provided by the media of mass communication have resulted in the now widespread belief that the incidence of child abuse, and its severity as a health and social problem, is on the increase, that it has, in fact, become a major cause of morbidity and mortality among children.[2] As is often the case with issues ranking high in public interest, however, systematic information on physical abuse of children continues to be scarce. The various claims concerning the nature and scope of this phenomenon are based on isolated observations and on several local, unrepresentative, clinical studies. Since each case of child abuse tends to upset the emotions of physicians, social workers, educators, police officers, judges, journalists, and others dealing with it, it is not surprising that distorted and exaggerated impressions and

1. U.S. Children's Bureau, Clearinghouse for Research in Child Life, *Bibliography on the Battered Child*, mimeographed (1966).
2. C. Henry Kempe et al., "The Battered-Child Syndrome," *Journal of the American Medical Association*, 181 (1962), 17–24.

opinions are formed concerning the nature and scope of the phenomenon as a social and health problem on the basis of isolated, unsystematic observations.

To reduce the lack in systematic knowledge concerning the quality and quantity of physical abuse of children in American society at this time, the Children's Bureau of the United States Department of Health, Education, and Welfare initiated in 1965 a series of nationwide studies. This book is a comprehensive report on these studies and their findings, and also presents an interpretation of the phenomenon as suggested by the findings.

The studies in this series include a nationwide survey of public knowledge, attitudes, and opinions about physical child abuse in the United States conducted during October 1965, nationwide press surveys of child-abuse incidents during 1965 and 1967, a pilot survey of child-abuse cases in California reported between September 1965 and February 1966 to the State Department of Justice, a survey of every incident of child abuse reported through legal channels throughout the entire United States in 1967 and 1968, and a comprehensive analysis of every incident reported through legal channels during 1967 in a sample of cities and counties. The entire series of studies was conducted within the Child Welfare Research Program of Brandeis University under a programmatic grant from the United States Children's Bureau. The National Opinion Research Center at the University of Chicago participated in the implementation of the public opinion survey, and health, welfare, and law enforcement authorities in all the states, Washington, D.C., Puerto Rico, and the Virgin Islands collected data for the surveys and the comprehensive analysis of reported incidents.

Numerous individuals and organizations participated, assisted, and advised during the planning, the gathering of data, and the analysis of this series of studies. To mention all of them is not feasible.

The impetus to this research program was provided by the Children's Bureau of the U. S. Department of Health, Education, and Welfare, and more specifically by Mrs. Katherine B. Oettinger, former Chief of the Bureau, Dr. Charles P. Gershenson, Director of the Division of Research, and Miss Jean Rubin, a special consultant on child abuse. The Children's Bureau not only initiated these studies and provided financial support for their execution, but also assisted with advice throughout the vicissitudes of implementation. Staff members of its Washington office as well as of its regional offices were always ready to help with our complex tasks.

These studies could not have been carried out without the closest cooperation of state and local welfare, health, and law enforcement authorities in all the states, Washington, D.C., Puerto Rico, and the Virgin Islands. Special thanks are due the many civil servants responsible for the central registries of child abuse in all the states, and the numerous physicians, hospital employees, social workers, judges, probation officers, and police officers who assisted in data collection for the basic surveys and for the comprehensive study in sample communities.

The National Opinion Research Center at the University of Chicago implemented the public opinion survey on child abuse. The help of its professional staff and of its interviewers throughout the country is gratefully acknowledged.

The patience, tact, charms, and skills of the three field directors of the studies, Miss Meg Brimlow, Mr. Douglas Deeley, and Mr. Albert Olsen, were major factors of our success. Thanks are also due Dr. John H. Noble, who served for one year as Associate Study Director, and Mr. Albert Boswell, who implemented the pilot survey in California.

Several persons served ably as research assistants and secretaries: Miss Dail Neugarten, Mrs. Fran Barker, Mrs. Bernadette Erikson, Mrs. Grace B. Olin, Mrs. Sarah E. Pace, Miss Ann Marie Chiasson, Mr. Bernard Gershenson, Miss Sondra Sweigman, Mrs. Shirley Norman, Mrs. Elsa Cascio, and Mrs. Virginia Normann. Their responsible attitude and commitment to their sometimes tiring tasks assured a high level of reliability in editing and processing data. Thanks are also due Miss Mary Hyde of the Harvard University Computing Center, who assisted in processing our voluminous data.

Charles I. Schottland and my colleagues on the faculty of the Florence Heller Graduate School for Advanced Studies in Social Welfare at Brandeis University were a source of support and encouragement. Ann Orlov, Editor for the Behavioral Sciences at Harvard University Press, stimulated the writing of this book long before there was anything to write and provided a constructive critique during the actual writing.

Special recognition is due the thousands of troubled families whose experiences and conflicts provided the raw material for these studies. It is hoped that their participation in this work will have contributed toward an increased understanding of violence against children in our society and toward the development of policies and measures aimed at the reduction of its incidence.

Finally, special thanks go to my wife, Eva, and our sons, Daniel and Gideon, who accepted an undue measure of neglect while I pursued the intricacies of violence against children in American society.

D.G.G.
Waltham, Massachusetts
Summer, 1969

Contents

List of Tables

Violence against Children

Chapter One

*Background and Theoretical
Considerations*

Children in American, and in many other societies, have always been subjected to a wide range of physical and nonphysical abuse by parents and other caretakers, including teachers and child care personnel, and indirectly by society as a whole. In the course of centuries, progress has been made in protecting the interest and well-being of children — in comparison with earlier periods when parents tended to wield absolute power over their offsprings' life and death and when children were frequently abandoned to die of exposure, legally bartered and sold, mutilated to enhance their appeal as beggars, or thrashed by schoolmasters with rods and the cat-o'-nine-tails. In spite of progress in strengthening the social and legal status and the protection of children, however, the problem of their physical abuse continues to be a cause of serious concern in present-day American society. The extent of this broad concern is reflected in the fact that since 1940 several hundreds of professional articles and books concerning this phenomenon have been published by roentgenologists, pediatricians, psychiatrists, educators, social workers, social and behavioral scientists, and lawyers. Numerous papers have been presented at professional conferences of social workers, lawyers, and physicians during recent years, and the daily press, popular periodicals, radio, and television have provided ample coverage throughout the past few decades.

The impetus for professional and public interest in physical abuse of children was provided in the forties by observations of roentgenologists of cases of unexplained multiple fractures of the long bones of young children found in conjuction with subdural hematomas (swelling or bleeding under the skull between the brain and its protective membrane). Subsequent intensive clinical studies of these strange cases by social workers, pediatricians, and psychiatrists in children's hospitals, clinics, and child protective agencies in many communities throughout the country led to the suspicion and eventual confirmation that these unexplained injuries of children were often inflicted by their own parents and caretakers. As a result of these and many other studies, physical abuse of children came to be viewed as a widespread and important medical and social problem, which often resulted in serious, irreversible damage to the physical well-being and emotional development of children and which sometimes even caused their death. The types of injuries inflicted upon children were found to range from minor, superficial bruises and cuts through burns, scaldings, fractures and internal injuries, to intentional starvation, dismemberment and severe injuries to the brain and central nervous system. The circumstances under which the injuries were inflicted were equally varied and ranged from simple disciplinary measures through uncontrollable angry outbursts, often under the influence of alcohol, to premeditated murderous attacks.

Opinions varied widely with respect to the etiology and dynamics of the phenomenon and the characteristics of individuals and families involved. Many investigators concluded that physical abuse of children was an expression of severe personality disorders on the part of the perpetrators who attacked the children in their care. Many students of the phenomenon also noted that severe disturbances of family relationships as well as environmental strains and stresses such as those related to life in poverty were significantly associated with incidents of child abuse. Finally, investigators also noted that some children, because of unusual congenital or acquired characteristics, may occasionally be more prone to provoking abusive attacks against themselves than other, more "normal" children. Definite knowledge as to the nature and scope of physical child abuse was lacking at the time the present series of studies was initiated, however, and widely differing views were held concerning the social, psychological, legal, and administrative treatment and handling of incidents of child abuse. Some professionals expressed optimistic views concerning the potential of therapeutic intervention with abusive parents, while others questioned seriously the value of such intervention, and suggested that emphasis be given to assuring the safety of the abused child by removing him from his family.

The growing awareness of, and the increasing interest in, the phenomenon of child abuse on the part of physicians, educators, social workers and lawyers, as well as of the public at large, led during the sixties to the enactment by all the states of laws requiring or recommending that medical personnel and others report incidents of suspected physical abuse of children to appropriate local and state authorities. The swift passage of these laws throughout the United States, in spite of controversy concerning details, was the result of an intensive promotional effort on the part of the United States Children's Bureau and many national, state and local professional and service organizations. A major objective of the reporting legislation was to improve mechanisms for case-finding and to assure protective services for the abused child, his siblings, and his parents. A secondary purpose was to gain a better understanding of the scope and nature of physical child abuse than was possible when only a few selected cases came to the notice of health, education, welfare, and law enforcement authorities. This purpose was pursued by the studies reported in this book.

The general approach of the studies to be reported in subsequent chapters was macroscopic and epidemiologic in contradistinction to the many clinically oriented studies of physical child abuse which were in progress or had already been completed when this series was initiated in 1965. The basic issues the present studies were designed to explore are the nature, dynamics, and scope of physical abuse of children in American society, its incidence rate in the total population, and its patterns of distribution among selected subsegments of the population. The ultimate purpose of these studies was to gain sufficient understanding of this phenomenon so that social policy recommendations could be developed aimed at the gradual reduction of its incidence and prevalence in American society.

More specifically, the studies examined the following issues:

a. Public knowledge, attitudes, and opinions about physical abuse of children in the United States;

b. Incidence of physical abuse of children in the entire population of the United States and in selected subsegments of this population;

c. Characteristics of victims, of perpetrators, and of families involved in incidents of child abuse;

d. Circumstances surrounding incidents of child abuse and the nature of injuries sustained by victims;

e. Health, welfare, and legal measures taken by authorities to whom reports on incidents are made in accordance with state laws;

f. Associations between selected variables included in the foregoing items.

An essential first step in investigating a phenomenon as complex as physical abuse of children is to develop an unambiguous definition as a basis for identifying and describing discrete incidents. Anyone who attempts a systematic exploration of physical child abuse in the United States is struck immediately by the difficulties encountered by scholars and professional workers in the field in their attempts to develop conceptual and operational definitions of this phenomenon, especially when one compares these difficulties with the relative simplicity and clarity of the definition of individual acts of violence directed against adult members of that same society. Books and articles dealing with child abuse reveal that nearly every investigator and author struggled with the problem of conceptual definition only to come up eventually with an unsatisfactory, more or less complex, relative, and ambiguous statement. One important reason for these difficulties seems to be that many investigators constructed definitions of child abuse in terms of the observed effects of an attack on a child, such as injuries sustained by him, rather than in terms of the motivation and behavior of the attacking person. Such definitions disregard the motivational and behavioral dynamics of perpetrators and result in vagueness, since the outcomes of violent, abusive acts depend not only on the perpetrator's behavior, but also on the victim's reaction to the perpetrator's behavior, and on environmental and chance circumstances.

For example, a father, angry at the misbehavior of his two sons, attacks them violently and throws one of them on a concrete floor and the other on a carpeted section of the same floor. The father's act, and apparently also his motivation, were identical with regard to both boys, yet the consequence of the act was serious physical injury to only one of them.

In an effort to minimize ambiguity in defining physical abuse of children, the following conceptual definition was developed; it is based on the behavior of perpetrators, rather than on the variable consequences of such behavior:

Physical abuse of children is the intentional, nonaccidental use of physical force, or intentional, nonaccidental acts of omission, on the part of a parent or other caretaker interacting with a child in his care, aimed at hurting, injuring, or destroying that child.

The foregoing definition seems sound conceptually, but is not completely satisfactory as an operational definition, for it may not always be possible to differentiate between intentional and accidental behavior. It should be noted also that the presence of intentional elements in the behavior of perpetrators does not imply complete absence of chance elements. On the contrary, many incidents of child abuse may involve a mix of intentional and chance elements and, at times, it may be impossible to determine the exact role played in a given incident by chance and that played by intentional behavior. An added difficulty is the fact that behavior which appears to be accidental may be determined in part by unconsciously intentional elements. Thus, while the boundary between pure accidents and physical abuse can be drawn clearly on a conceptual level, it may, at times, be difficult to differentiate between them without thorough examination of the motivations that underlie manifest behavior in given incidents.

Apart from the difficulty of ascertaining the presence of elements of intentionality, which, by definition, constitute a sine qua non of child abuse, the definition suggested here reduces ambiguity by including *all* use of physical force and *all* acts of omission aimed at hurting, injuring, or destroying a child, irrespective of the degree of seriousness of the act, the omission, and/or the outcome. Thus the relativity of personal and community standards and judgments is avoided in the definition.

Sexual abuse of a child in one's care is not included in the present definition of physical child abuse unless it also involves the use of physical force against the child. This means that a child who is abused sexually without resistance is not a victim of physical abuse as defined here. The exclusion of pure sexual abuse from the definition of physical child abuse is based on the assumption that perpetrators of sexual abuse are motivated differently from perpetrators of physical abuse. The former seem to seek primarily sexual self-gratification, while the latter seem primarily intent upon hurting the child. The two phenomena are likely to differ in their dynamics and should, therefore, be studied apart from each other.

The inclusion in the definition of physical child abuse of intentional acts of omission, such as intentional withholding of food, may also lead to certain diagnostic difficulties, since acts of omission which are due to neglect, ignorance, or lack of resources may produce physical consequences similar or identical to those resulting from acts of intentional omission. Here, too, however, the difficulty in differentiation is not conceptual but merely operational, and with proper examination of specific incidents it is usually possible to establish the presence or absence of intentional elements in acts of omission.

The term "caretaker" in the definition refers to a person who functioned in a de facto child-caring role for the child whom he abused. The child-caring role is not defined quantitatively by duration in time but qualitatively by the nature of the constellation existing between the child and the person at the time of the abusive incident. This constellation involves elements of actual or presumed responsibility for maintaining or guarding the child's well-being and welfare.

The aforementioned consistent difficulty of scholars and practitioners to agree upon an unambiguous, simple definition of child abuse similar to the one suggested here indicates that the problem may not be merely one of focus, logic, and semantics. Rather, it would seem that this difficulty reflects the ambivalent and ambiguous attitudes of American society with respect to children and to child-rearing philosophies and practices.

Chapter One

When an adult person uses physical force in interaction with another adult person in order to hurt, injure, or destroy him, such behavior is considered simply as assault, battery, murder, etc., and human societies maintain strong taboos, and correspondingly strong legal sanctions, against the use of physical force in such interaction. Employment of physical force between adults in society tends to be strictly limited and regulated. It is reserved usually for specially established societal institutions such as the police and the military, and may be used even by these institutions only under clearly specified conditions. These universal, cultural taboos and legal sanctions against the use of physical force in interpersonal relations among adults seem to have evolved out of the recognition of man at the dawn of civilization that there exists an approximate balance of physical force between each adult individual and every other adult individual; that, hence, the chance of hurting and of being hurt in a physical encounter between adults was about even; and that, therefore, forsaking the use of physical force in interaction between adult members of a society would increase the chance of survival for all.

The range and quality of cultural taboos and legal sanctions concerning the use of physical force in the interaction between adults and children are very different from those regulating the use of physical force in the interaction among adults. Most societies, including American society, with the possible exception of certain American Indian tribes, have not developed absolute cultural taboos and legal sanctions against the use of physical force against children by adults. Not only is such use of physical force not prohibited, but it is even encouraged in specified contexts by many societies. The educational philosophy reflected in the popular proverb "spare the rod and spoil the child" is still widely accepted throughout civilized societies. Moreover, children were considered the property of their parents in many societies, and parents had, thus, absolute power over their life and death. Teachers, too, at their discretion, had, and still have, the right to use physical force against their students for purposes of teaching and discipline.[1] Courts under the law, did, and still do, sentence children to corporal punishment,[2] and many institutions whose stated function it is to care for and rehabilitate children attempt to do so by means of physical force.[3] Children throughout history have often been mutilated for economic gain or ritualistic objectives. Infanticide was practiced by many societies as a means of population control, to eliminate undesirable offspring, or for sacrificial purposes. Children were also sold as slaves or forced to work in agriculture or industry under most inhumane conditions.[4]

While with the passage of time society's interest in and protection of the needs and rights of children have made considerable

1. See, e.g., Jonathan Kozol, *Death at an Early Age* (Boston, Houghton Mifflin, 1967).

2. A news item from the *New York Times* of March 27, 1969, illustrates the point: "Oklahoma City, March 26 (UPI) — A judge's decision to let a teen-age lawbreaker choose between five years in prison and 20 lashes with a belt is being investigated by the Federal Bureau of Investigation. F.B.I. agents questioned District Court Judge Carmon C. Harris Tuesday and have been talking with other court employes involved in the case of Scott Browning Grandstaff, 17 years old, who chose the whipping over prison on Dec. 21. Grandstaff, who pleaded guilty to charges of possession of stolen property, had two suspended sentences on burglary charges on his record when Judge Harris said to him: 'Corporal punishment has gone out of style, and you probably have never received any at home. That is the reason you are in this predicament.' The boy's mother stood in the judge's chambers as a male relative gave Grandstaff 20 whacks with a belt. The boy's father is an invalid." From the *Times* of August 17, 1969, Judge Vincent A. Carroll, of Philadelphia, urging a crackdown on teen-age gangs: "We should bring back the old days of the whipping post. That's what these gang members need. They should be humiliated right on the public streets, with whippings, in front of the people they've been terrorizing."

3. See the series of fifteen articles by Howard James, "Children in Trouble," in the weekend issues of the *Christian Science Monitor* starting on March 29, 1969, and the editorial "The Unnecessary Scandal" in the same issue — published in book form by David McKay, 1970.

4. S. X. Radbill, "A History of Child Abuse and Infanticide," in Ray E. Helfer and C. Henry Kempe, eds., *The Battered Child* (Chicago, University of Chicago Press, 1968).

progress,[5] and individual and societal physical violence against children decreased, such violence still constitutes a widely sanctioned phenomenon in American society at the present stage of its cultural development. That this is indeed still the case is reflected in formally codified sanctions such as the discretional right of teachers in many states to administer corporal punishment to children.[6] It is also reflected in cultural values, traditions, and customs, and in actual child-rearing practices throughout the United States, all of which uphold the discretional right of parents and other caretakers of children to use a "reasonable amount of physical force" in disciplining children. It is finally reflected in the conflicting and ambiguous attitudes, interpretations and actions of professionals and agencies in the fields of health, education, welfare, religion and law enforcement when dealing with issues and problems in the relationship of parents and children, and more specifically in the just-mentioned difficulties concerning the conceptual definition of physical abuse of children and appropriate ways of dealing with it.

The marked differences in cultural values, traditions, and customs, and in legal sanctions concerning the use of physical force in interaction between adults and adults on the one hand, and adults and children on the other, seem to have evolved from certain biological realities and their psychological and social concomitants. The physical strength of adults exceeds that of children to such an extent that the chance of an adult being hurt in a physical encounter with a child is quite negligible. Thus, in terms of the survival needs of adults, there has never existed a compelling necessity for the development of sanctions against the use of physical force in adult-child interaction. There certainly

5. Dorothy M. Jones, *Children Who Need Protection — An Annotated Bibliography* (Washington, D.C., Government Printing Office, 1966).

6. It is interesting to note that several state legislatures enacted laws permitting teachers to use corporal punishment at the same legislative session at which they enacted a law mandating the reporting of physical abuse of children.

existed a necessity for such sanctions in terms of the survival needs of children. The survival needs of children, however, seem to have been a less decisive factor in the evolution of cultural values and sanctions than those of adults, and it is thus understandable that values and sanctions against the use of physical force against children remained vague and weak, or did not evolve at all. Next is the fact that children, being the biological offspring of their parents, tended to be considered their property as well as their responsibility. This meant that parents had a wide range of rights and discretion in the treatment of their children and were also given the task of socializing them. This allocation of the socialization function to the family seems to be a further reason for condoning the use of physical force against children by parents, since the socialization situation is invariably structured in a manner that bestows dominant status, rights, and power upon the adult, and subordinate status and minimal rights and power upon the child. As these societal arrangements are experienced as "natural" consequences of biological realities, they tend to become internalized in the personalities of each new generation, with the result that members of society tend to accept the appropriateness of discretional use of physical force toward children by parents and other adults who act in loco parentis, or to whom certain aspects of the socialization function are delegated.

One may therefore conclude that a certain measure of physical abuse of children is a fully sanctioned aspect of the current stage of cultural development of American society. There exist significant differences between various segments of the American population concerning the extent of physical abuse of children which is considered appropriate, and which is actually practiced. In spite of such differences, however, it cannot be denied that some measure of violence against children is patterned into the child-rearing philosophies and practices of nearly all Americans. In view of this situation the existing difficulties surrounding the conceptual definition of child abuse should surprise no one, for a definition, to be valid, cannot be based upon subjective judgments of the severity of observed effects. Because of these difficulties in defining physical abuse, it is a very frustrating task to obtain accurate figures on the incidence and prevalence of this phenomenon. Estimates of various investigators range from a few thousand to several million incidents per year.

With a sociocultural frame of reference in hand, one may turn to the apparent scientific conflict between psychodynamic and sociocultural conceptualizations. Most investigators who conducted intensive clinical studies of abusive parents and their child-victims concluded that violent, destructive attacks on children tend to result from complicated personality disorders of the abusive parents, and at times also of the abused children, as well as from interpersonal relationship problems in the families, and from environmental stress. The emphasis on sociocultural factors is not intended to question the validity of these clinical findings, but to give them a broader perspective. For it seems that the manner in which individual personality disorders are expressed, and the content of neurotic and psychotic fantasies and symptoms in any given society, tend to be influenced by the sociocultural context in which they develop. Such disorders, fantasies, and symptoms tend to be extreme manifestations of attitudes and behaviors which, at a less extreme level, constitute a normal element of the culture and are sanctioned by it. In other words, what a society considers sick and deviant in human behavior is not necessarily qualitatively different from what it considers healthy and normal. The difference may be quantitative only. Thus it would seem that incidents of serious physical attack on children which can be understood dynamically as symptoms of individual psychological disorders and/or environmental stress may at the same time be deeply rooted in culturally supported attitudes. Consequently, it is possible that a society that unambiguously rejected the use of physical force against children would have a lower rate of emotionally sick individuals whose symptomatology involved destructive behavior toward children than would a society that does not reject such use of physical force.

The preceding argument suggests that sociocultural and psychodynamic conceptualizations of child abuse do not negate but supplement each other. The phenomenon of physical abuse of children can, therefore, be conceived to range over a wide spectrum. At one end are incidents involving neither personality deviance nor environmental stress. The perpetrators in these incidents are normal individuals who are acting in a manner approved by their culture while disciplining children in their care. The undesirable outcome of their actions may be due to chance factors, but the dynamic source underlying their behavior is a culturally determined attitude. On the other extreme end of the spectrum are incidents involving individuals who suffer from various types of personality disorders and whose abusive attacks on children in their care are triggered by these disorders in various combinations with environmental stress factors. In these cases, too, however, culturally determined attitudes concerning child-rearing are likely to be elements in the etiology of the personality disorders, since symptoms of such disorders tend to be exaggerated manifestations of culturally approved behavior. Between these extremes of the spectrum, cases can be conceived of as ordered along a continuum of ascending personality deviance and environmental stress superimposed throughout on culturally determined attitudes. This model shows that a psychodynamic interpretation of physical abuse of children explains only an extreme segment of a much wider socioculturally determined spectrum. These extreme cases can also be viewed as psychologically determined deviations from a culturally determined normal range of violence against children.

It is not surprising that investigators who conducted clinically oriented studies of physical child abuse in hospitals and child-protective agencies tend to emphasize psychodynamic factors of the phenomenon, since the more deviant segment of the total spectrum is likely to be overrepresented in study samples drawn from hospital and agency populations. As will be shown in a later chapter, if, in studying physical child abuse, the sampling frame is broadened so as to include a less narrowly defined universe, the ratio of psychologically normal to psychologically deviant personalities among the population of abusive parents changes significantly, and the majority turn out to be within the normal range.

Since, as has been suggested, the use of physical force against children is such a widespread, culturally sanctioned phenomenon in American society, one cannot avoid raising the question whether there exists a connection between exposure to violence in childhood at the hand of one's parents, and infliction of violence on one's children as an adult. Furthermore, one may wonder whether the widespread phenomenon of adult violence in American society may be indirectly related to the exposure to physical violence of a large segment of the population during childhood. These questions cannot be answered reliably without extensive longitudinal, experimental studies. Some clues to answers of the questions are available, however. It is known that in many instances perpetrators of child abuse have been themselves victims of abuse during their own childhood. It is also known that children often tend to pattern their behavior after their parents' behavior. Thus parents and other caretakers, like teachers, who use physical force in interaction with children, may teach by example that physical force is a legitimate modality for social interaction. Since children are thus taught through experience that violence is sanctioned in some interpersonal contexts but not in others, they are exposed to conflicting signals, or to double standards, and they may grow up with an almost unsolvable conflict in their system of values according to which violence is both right and wrong, good and bad.

Although the studies reported in this volume are concerned with physical abuse of children as individual acts of violence, some comments seem indicated here on a related issue. In American society culturally sanctioned individual acts of violence against children within the family and within institutionalized settings of socialization are paralleled, and perhaps exceeded in intensity and impact, by what must be considered "collective, societal abuse" of large segments of the young generation. American society has sometimes been described as child centered; however, any unbiased observer of child life in this nation will find that many millions of children are living and growing up under circumstances of severe social and economic deprivation which tend to inhibit the fullest possible development of their innate capacities, since they affect negatively their physical, social, intellectual and emotional development. Many of these children lack adequate nutrition, medical and dental care, and educational and vocational opportunities. For many of them developmental opportunities have been severely limited since birth. Poverty and various forms of discrimination constitute perhaps the most inhumane and most persistent form of violence and abuse perpetrated against the young generation of this nation, and the one for which society is paying the highest penalty in terms of lost human potential and of long-range socioeconomic costs. The relationship between growing up under conditions of poverty and discrimination and crimes of violence during adolescence and adulthood has been noticed by many investigators. The present series of studies revealed also a significant association between growing up in poverty and being subjected to acts of individual violence and abuse. In other words, individual acts of violence against children tend to be associated with collective violence against them, and it therefore seems that society's violence against its young generation in the form of poverty and discrimination may constitute an important aspect of the violence syndrome or the "cycle of violence."

Two further questions need to be raised and examined here: (a) Why has physical abuse of children stirred up so much professional, governmental, and general public interest and concern in recent years? (b) Why do the mass media of communication and the general public accept so readily an interpretation according to which physical abuse of children is caused by some form of emotional disturbance or sickness on the part of individual perpetrators? The answers are not known, though some educated guesses may be attempted. One possible answer to the first question may be related to the issue of collective, societal abuse of children. Awareness of this version of child abuse has increased during recent decades, but as a society Americans have done little to overcome poverty, discrimination, and deprivation and their disastrous effects upon millions of their children. Any serious student of child life in American society would have to conclude that, however high the prevalence of physical abuse of individual children within their families and homes may be, the abuse inflicted upon children collectively by society as a whole is far larger in scope and far more serious in its consequences. Yet public and professional concern with child abuse in individual homes tends to exceed by far the concern with this massive, collective abuse of children by society as a whole. Could it be that the oversensationalized interest in the former phenomenon serves as a smoke screen to cover up society's destructive inaction with respect to the latter? Are abusive parents perhaps seized upon as convenient scapegoats to expiate society's collective guilt for abusing countless numbers of its young?

The explanation suggested here for the intensive public interest in child abuse is derived from social psychology, but there is an alternative explanation derived from individual psychology. Abusive parents may serve as scapegoats not only for society's collective guilt but also for the individual guilt experienced by many parents as a result of aggressive impulses and fantasies toward their children. Such aggressive impulses and fantasies may be a rather common experience of parents in the course of rearing children, yet they are in conflict with the ideal of constant parental love, and many parents may, therefore, tend to deny and repress such feelings and to react to them with a vague sense of guilt. Their interest in reports on child-abuse incidents and their self-righteous outrage against parents who lost their self-control and succumbed to such aggressive impulses and fantasies may be a convenient mechanism for relieving their own sense of guilt.

As for the second question, is it possible that the illness-as-cause hypothesis is accepted readily because it soothes society's conscience, as well as the conscience of individual parents who may be subject to abusive impulses? Society is absolved from guilt by this interpretation, for if child abuse is the result of the emotional illness of the perpetrators, social conditions need not be blamed, society is justified in the self-righteous prosecution of individual perpetrators, and it need not examine the social circumstances and cultural trends which may be major factors of child abuse. Individual parents, too, may derive gratification from the sickness-as-cause interpretation, since it may fill them with a sense of security. For if abusive behavior were a function of sickness, most parents could view themselves as free from the danger of falling prey to it, since they do not consider themselves sick.

This examination of the widespread, intensive, public and personal interest in physical abuse of children, and of the all-too-ready acceptance of the sickness-as-cause hypothesis, suggests the conclusion that both these phenomena may be highly functional mechanisms, since they provide relief for the conscience of society as a whole and for the conscience of many individual parents.

Chapter Two

The Literature, and Legal and Professional Developments

The growing interest in physical abuse of children in the United States is reflected in the literature of medicine, law, and social welfare, as well as in publications addressed to the general public. A bibliography on child abuse compiled in 1966 by the U.S. Children's Bureau listed nearly 200 books and articles in professional and popular journals.[1] Since that time additional articles and books have been published. Collecting and reviewing this steadily growing body of printed material is, by now, a rather formidable task, and several recent reviews of the literature have been geared to the specialized interests of physicians, lawyers, psychologists, and social workers.[2]

---

1. *Bibliography on the Battered Child,* mimeographed.
2. Allan H. McCoid, "The Battered Child and Other Assaults upon the Family: Part One," *Minnesota Law Review,* 50 (1965), 1–58. Morris T. Paulson and Phillip R. Blake, "The Abused, Battered and Maltreated Child: A Review," *Trauma,* 9 (1967), 1–136. Larry B. Silver, "Child Abuse Syndrome: A Review," *Medical Times,* 96 (1968), 803–818. Serapio R. Zalba, "The Abused Child: I, A Survey of the Problem," *Social Work,* 11 (1966), 3–16.

John Caffey, a specialist in pediatric radiology, was perhaps first among medical authors to draw attention to certain unexplainable injuries observed in young children. In an article published in 1946 he discussed several cases involving multiple fractures of the long bones of infants in various stages of healing associated with subdural hematomas.[3] Though Dr. Caffey suspected that the conditions he observed were traumatic in origin, he did not attempt to identify their sources. His suspicions were supported by observations published by other radiologists in subsequent years, one of whom, F. N. Silverman, suspected parental carelessness but not intentionally abusive behavior.[4] P. V. Woolley and W. A. Evans were the first medical authors who attributed the skeletal lesions to possibly intentional acts of parents or others caring for the children.[5] Dr. Caffey re-examined his earlier observations in 1957 and at that time reached the conclusion that trauma, willfully inflicted by parents, may have caused the conditions he had described in 1946.[6] Similar conclusions were reached and reported on by several medical authors during the late fifties. All these writers recommended the use of X rays in combination with detailed case histories and descriptions of the circumstances surrounding the injuries as diagnostic tools for uncovering clues to parental abuse.[7]

3. *American Journal of Roentgenology*, 56 (1946), 163–173.
4. "The Roentgen Manifestations of Unrecognized Skeletal Trauma in Infants," *American Journal of Roentgenology, Radium Therapy and Nuclear Medicine*, 69 (1953), 413–427.
5. "Significance of Skeletal Lesions in Infants Resembling Those of Traumatic Origin," *Journal of the American Medical Association*, 158 (1955), 539–543.
6. "Some Traumatic Lesions in Growing Bones Other Than Fractures and Dislocations — Clinical and Radiological Features," *British Journal of Radiology*, 30 (1957), 225–238.
7. S. and H. Fisher, "Skeletal Manifestations of Parent-Induced Trauma in Infants and Children," *Southern Medical Journal*, 51 (1958), 956–960. Henry K. Silver and C. Henry Kempe, "The Problem of Parental Criminal Neglect and Severe Physical Abuse of Children," *American Journal of Diseases of Children*, 98 (1959), 528. D. S. Miller, "Fractures among Children: Parental Assault as Causative Agent," *Minnesota Medicine*, 42 (1959), 1209–1213, 1414–1425.

Once roentgenologists and pediatricians had identified abuse
inflicted by parents as a possible cause of serious physical injuries of children and had developed diagnostic case-finding procedures, social workers in children's hospitals became concerned
with the implications of this phenomenon for their practice. Elizabeth Elmer, at the Children's Hospital in Pittsburgh, was among
the first to discuss this subject.[8] She noted the difficulties of professionals to maintain an objective and helpful attitude toward
parents who abuse their children and drew attention to society's
repugnance for the phenomenon of child abuse, which, she
thought, was a factor in the reluctance of many physicians to
accept the diagnostic impressions of radiologists.

Complications inherent in comprehensive, interdisciplinary
case management of physically abused children were discussed
in a paper by Helen Boardman of the Children's Hospital in
Los Angeles.[9] The reluctance of abusive parents to admit attacks
on their children, their tendency to repeat such attacks when
children are returned home after hospitalization, and difficulties
in obtaining legally valid evidence in instances of child abuse
were viewed by Mrs. Boardman and her medical colleagues as
sources of complications in treatment and case management. In
spite of these complications, however, the staff of the Los Angeles Children's Hospital attempted to develop cooperative, interdisciplinary procedures to provide treatment and services for
abused children and their parents, who, too, were thought to be
in need of protection from the consequences of their own uncontrolled behavior.

C. Henry Kempe, a pediatrician at the University of Colorado
School of Medicine, and several of his colleagues published in
1962 an article in which they coined the term "the battered-child

8. "Abused Young Children Seen in Hospitals," *Social Work,* 5 (1960),
98–102.
9. "A Project to Rescue Children from Inflicted Injuries," *Social Work,*
7 (1962), 43–51.

syndrome." [10] The authors presented findings of a study of child-abuse incidents reported by 71 hospitals and 77 district attorneys from all over the United States. Many of the children of the 302 hospital cases and 447 cases known to district attorneys had died or had been seriously injured, and the authors concluded that physical abuse was a major cause of death and maiming of children. Many of the abusive parents were found to suffer from various types of personality disorders. The article discussed also the reluctance of physicians to believe in the possibility of parental abuse, and their reluctance to take on an investigative role. The authors recommended that physicians report all incidents which come to their attention to law-enforcement authorities or to child-protective agencies. The *Journal of the American Medical Association* commented favorably in an editorial on Dr. Kempe's article and recommended that doctors be alert to "battered baby" cases and cooperate with law enforcment agencies. [11]

Dr. Kempe's study and paper were presented to a group of lawyers, doctors, and social workers at a conference on child abuse called in 1962 by the U.S. Children's Bureau. The purpose was to plan steps aimed at reducing the prevalence of physical abuse. [12] The conference recommended the drafting of a model child-abuse reporting statute and an intensive effort to obtain the enactment of such statutes in all the states. [13] It may be noted that this effort was highly successful. By June 1967 every state in the United States had adopted laws which require, or recommend to, physicians and certain others to report suspected cases of child abuse to appropriate law enforcement or welfare author-

10. *Journal of the American Medical Association,* 181 (1962), 17–24.
11. Volume 181, p. 42.
12. "Report of Meeting on Physical Abuse of Infants and Young Children," unpublished (1962).
13. *The Abused Child: Principles and Suggested Language for Legislation on Reporting the Physically Abused Child* (Washington, D.C., Government Printing Office, 1963).

ities, and which free reporting persons from civil and criminal liability for doing so. According to Monrad G. Paulsen, Dean of the Law School at the University of Virginia, "few legislative proposals in the history of the United States have been so widely adopted in so little time." [14]

In 1962 the Massachusetts Society for the Prevention of Cruelty to Children published findings of a statewide study of child abuse.[15] This study examined the cases of 180 abused children from 115 families who had been reported to the agency during 1960. The median age of the children was 7. The families of the children were found to suffer from a variety of interpersonal difficulties and were not integrated into their communities. The parents revealed a wide range of personality disorders, and their relationships with the children whom they had abused were severely disturbed. Frequently, one specific child in a family appeared to be singled out as a victim. Legal, medical, and psychiatric implications of this study were discussed in separate papers in the same publication. The importance of interdisciplinary cooperation in dealing with cases of child abuse was stressed by all the authors.

Another study published at about the same time was a nationwide survey of the press conducted by the Children's Division of the American Humane Association.[16] During 1962 the Association had collected press reports on 662 cases of child abuse, including 178 fatalities. Most of the reported children were under 4 years old. Over 70 percent had been abused by their parents, and fathers were responsible for the more severe injuries. Abuse by fathers resulted primarily from uncontrolled outbursts while disciplining a child. Maternal abuse tended to result from the

14. "Legal Protections against Child Abuse," *Children,* 13 (1966), 42–48.

15. Edgar J. Merrill, "Physical Abuse of Children — An Agency Study," in *Protecting the Battered Child* (Denver, Col., American Humane Association, 1962).

16. Vincent DeFrancis, *Child Abuse — Preview of a Nationwide Survey* (Denver, Col., American Humane Association, 1963).

mothers' deep-seated emotional problems. Most families seemed affected by a wide range of internal problems, and most parents seemed emotionally immature. In about 20 percent of the families there was no father living at home.

Subsequent to the publication of this survey the American Humane Association issued in 1963 its own guidelines for legislation concerning mandatory reporting of physical abuse of children,[17] which were similar to the Children's Bureau guidelines. Although the Children's Bureau suggested that the police should receive reports of child abuse, the Humane Association recommended that reports be made to child protective agencies.

In 1963 the Child Welfare League of America published a collection of papers by medical social workers, a physician, and a nurse entitled *The Neglected Battered-Child Syndrome*.[18] The subtitle of this pamphlet, "Role Reversal in Parents," reflected the attempt of the authors to develop a psychiatric conceptualization of child abuse. According to Marian G. Morris and Robert W. Gould of the Children's Hospital in Philadelphia, an abusing parent views his victim not as the child he really is but as his own parent, who has failed, hurt, and frustrated him. The abuse is intended for that "absent parent" but is displaced and acted out against the helpless present child. The child in such cases is expected by the parent to meet his (the parent's) complex emotional needs, rather than having his needs met by the parent; when the child fails to do so, the frustrated parent attacks, injures, and at times destroys the child. Morris and her colleagues explored also differences in the behavior of abusive and nonabusive parents, and of abused and nonabused children.[19] The purpose of these explorations was to provide medical and social-welfare personnel with diagnostic clues that would aid in

17. American Humane Association, *Guidelines for Legislation to Protect the Battered Child* (Denver, Col., 1963).

18. New York, 1963.

19. Marian G. Morris, Robert W. Gould, and Patricia J. Matthews, "Toward Prevention of Child Abuse," *Children*, 11 (1964), 55–60.

case finding, in the planning of treatment for individual cases, and in preventing recidivism.

Studies by social workers of characteristics of abusive parents and abused children, and of differences between them and neglectful parents and their children, continued to be published throughout the 1960's. Leontine Young completed a study involving 142 cases known to several child-protective agencies,[20] Shirley Nurse published findings of an intensive study of twenty abusive families known to the Juvenile Court in New York City,[21] and Elizabeth Elmer and her medical colleagues published results of a longitudinal, clinical, medical-social investigation of fifty abusive families known to the Children's Hospital in Pittsburgh.[22] All these studies found qualitative differences between abusive and nonabusive parents, and also suggested that many abusive parents had been abused by their own parents during childhood. Similar observations had been reported some fifteen years earlier by Eustace Chesser, who found cruelty toward children related to deep-seated pyschological deviations of the perpetrators which could often be traced to physical and mental cruelty inflicted upon them during childhood by their own parents.[23]

James Delsordo published in 1963 findings of a study of eighty cases of abused children who had been reported to the Pennsylvania Society to Protect Children from Cruelty.[24] The purpose of this study had been not only to describe the cases but to develop a typology of abusive parents which could guide treat-

20. "The Behavior Syndrome of Parents Who Neglect and Abuse Their Children," dissertation (Columbia University, 1963). L. R. Young, *Wednesday's Children* (New York, McGraw-Hill, 1964).

21. "Familial Patterns of Parents Who Abuse Their Children," *Smith College Studies in Social Work,* 35 (1964), 11–25.

22. Thomas McHenry, Bertram R. Girdany, and Elizabeth Elmer, "Unsuspected Trauma with Multiple Skeletal Injuries during Infancy and Childhood," *Pediatrics,* 31 (1963), 903–908.

23. *Cruelty to Children* (New York, Philosophical Library, 1952).

24. "Protective Casework for Abused Children," *Children,* 10 (1963), 213–218.

ment, especially with reference to the question of removing an abused child from his parents' custody or leaving him in their care. Five types were identified in this study:

1. abuse resulting from "parents' acute mental illness"

2. abuse as "an overflow from the parents' aimless way of life"

3. "a non-specific disturbance in the parent resulting in severe battering of the child"

4. abuse due to "parents' harshness in disciplining children"

5. abuse due to "parents' misplaced conflicts"

In spite of its crudeness this typology was useful for practice decisions. The author recommended that children be removed from the care of abusive parents of the first three types.

Serapio R. Zalba[25] published in 1967 a more systematic typology of child abuse based on the locus of the problem and the parents' ability to control abusive behavior in the future. The six types identified by Zalba are shown in the table on page 26. Zalba suggested that children should not be left in the custody of parents belonging to the first three types, but could be left with parents belonging to types 4 through 6, provided the parents receive appropriate treatment.

Perhaps the most consistent effort toward psychiatric understanding has been made at the University of Colorado Medical School by Brandt F. Steele and his colleagues. Dr. Steele collaborated with Dr. Kempe in the already cited study which led in 1962 to the publication of "The Battered-Child Syndrome" [26] and since that time has conducted intensive studies and undertaken the treatment of families involved in abusing children.

In 1966 Drs. Steele and Kempe sponsored a workshop on physical abuse of children in which investigators from all over

25. "The Abused Child: II, A Typology for Classification and Treatment," *Social Work*, 12 (1967), 70–79.

26. See above, note 10.

Classification of Abusive Parents (Zalba)

Locus of Problem	Parent's Ability to Control Abuse	
	Not able to control	Able to control
Personality System	1. Psychotic parent	
	2. Pervasively angry and abusive parent	
	3. Depressive, passive-aggressive parent	4. Cold, compulsive disciplinarian parent
Family System		5. Impulsive but generally adequate parent with marital conflict
Person-Environment or Family-Environment System		6. Parent with identity/role crisis

the United States participated. Most participants were psychiatrists, pediatricians, and social workers, and interpretations of child abuse offered at the institute were derived primarily from psychiatric theory. Irving Kaufman, a practicing psychiatrist and consultant to social agencies in Boston, summarized his observations at the workshop as follows: "Regardless of the core fantasy associated with the parent's attack upon the child, the point in time at which the attack occurs requires a major distortion in reality for the parent to be able to carry out a brutal assault on a child. The child is no longer perceived as helpless, dependent on his parents for love, care, and nurturance, but as some symbolic referent upon whom the assault is launched." [27] In an earlier paper Dr. Kaufman had reached the following conclusion concerning the personality of abusive parents: "This type of vio-

27. "Proceedings of Conference on Patterns of Parental Behavior Leading to Physical Abuse of Children," unpublished (University of Colorado, School of Medicine, 1966).

lent, abusive behavior is associated with some type of unreality. In its most extreme form it is associated with a type of schizophrenic process. Although many of these parents are not continuously or overtly schizophrenic, many of these individuals who have episodic outbursts of loss of control, loss of reason and loss of judgment represent a type of schizophrenia . . . Attacking a child is a crime of violence, and some of the persons who get so violently out of control may fall into the category of the antisocial schizophrenic." [28]

In the same paper Dr. Kaufman commented also on the transmission of the abusive pattern from parents to children:

As a further component to the consideration of the impact of this type of parent as an identification figure for their children, we found in a current research project[29] studying childhood schizophrenia that the antisocial type of schizophrenic tended to come from this type of disruptive home with such violent abusive parents who demonstrated uncontrolled aggressive and sexual behavior, and who were unrelated to the community. These were parents who themselves had a psychotic core in that their basic anxieties were related to fears of annihilation which they handled by externalizing and attacking.

Richard Galdston, a psychiatrist at the Children's Hospital in Boston who had studied and treated abusive parents and their children for several years, presented the following interpretations of the psychodynamics of abusive parents at the University of Colorado workshop:

28. "Psychiatric Implications of Physical Abuse of Children," in *Protecting the Battered Child,* pp. 17–22.

29. Here the author cites Kaufman et al., "Four Types of Defense in Mothers and Fathers of Schizophrenic Children," *American Journal of Orthopsychiatry,* 29 (1959), 460–472.

The Syndrome is viewed as the result of a parent's attempt to cope with internal conflict by means of externalization, utilizing a particular child as a partial personal representation.

The following factors collectively dispose parents to resort to the physical abuse of children in order to spare themselves the conscious experience of their own intra-psychic distress.

1. Major reliance upon projection as a leading defense against intra-psychic stress . . . There is a defect in their capacity to test the reality of the child. The child functions as a delusion in what is essentially a transference psychosis.
2. A tendency to translate affect states into physical activity without intervention of conscious thought.
3. The presence of intolerable self-hatred: This is the "it" which the parent "takes out" on the child . . . tries to dispose of . . . by projecting . . . onto the child and exorcising . . . through physical abuse. The child is the scapegoat for the parent's unconscious sense of guilt.
4. Correspondence of the child by sex, age and position in the family to events in the parent's own life which occasioned . . . great self-hatred . . . It is the presence of the child of a particular sex, age and position which serves as the seed crystal about which the parent's forgotten unwanted emotions threaten to precipitate out of unconsciousness into awareness.
5. Relative lack of available alternative modes of defense against conflict because of environmental factors: Poverty, illness, domestic demands, social isolation, housing problems all can contribute an increment to the likelihood of physical abuse by reducing the availability of alternative modes for discharging intra-psychic tensions.

6. Compliance with the act of abuse by the marriage partner due to dependence and a reciprocal willingness to
support projective defenses . . .
7. Relative absence of available authority figures: The de-
terrent power of grandparents, religious or social authorities as an antidote to idiosyncratic perceptions and
eccentric behavior is seldom available to the abusive
parent.

Irvin D. Milowe, a psychiatrist at Children's Hospital in Washington, D.C., another participant at the workshop, expressed
some skepticism concerning the extent of psychiatric understanding of physical abuse of children which can be considered as
established knowledge. He was the first to suggest that children
themselves may in certain situations contribute to their own
abuse, and he also pointed to the intergenerational dimension of
abusive child-rearing patterns. Excerpts from Dr. Milowe's comments at the workshop follow:

Our information about the personality patterns of parents
who batter their children remains largely anecdotal. Similar
life circumstances and dynamics coexist in other parents who
do not batter their children and we are unable to quantify
our studies of the interrelationship between ego strength,
life stress, intensity of sadistic impulses and resultant battering . . . Primitive personality fixations, or massive regres-
sions, coupled with specific needs of the child, are seen to
frequently interlock and where reality pressures are crushing,
capacity to control rage because of love of the child or
through supportive relationships reduced, such impulses are
acted out . . . The parent's childhood loads the gun; present life conflicts cause the parent to raise it; the child's phase-
specific needs help pull the trigger. . . . Some (and it may
only be a small percentage) of these infants are atypically

difficult and irritating children. Some have described a particularly grating quality to their crying; nurses and social workers have confessed understanding why a parent might batter "THAT CHILD." Indeed, reports confirm that some of these children get battered in sequential foster home placements where no other child has ever been battered . . . There are indications that some batterings occur *only* when specific developmental stages in the child trigger specific conflicts in the parent and not at earlier or later times. . . . In some families such violence can be traced through at least three generations.

Brandt Steele, cosponsor of the workshop, questioned some of the interpretations offered by his psychiatric colleagues. Based on intensive studies and treatment of sixty abusive families which he and his collaborators at the University of Colorado Medical School had conducted over four years they concluded that the broad range of personality disturbances that had been found in association with child abuse occurred also with persons who did not abuse their children. Thus it was not possible to view these conditions as sufficient causal explanations of child abuse. Some of Dr. Steele's observations at the workshop follow:

> Four years of studying the abuse of children by their caretakers have led us to consider one hypothesis as basic to the problem; namely, that we are dealing with a certain pattern of child rearing.
>
> Abuse is a pattern of interaction between caretaker and child that is unusual because of the intensity in the expression of the pattern. The pattern itself, we are convinced, is pervasive in our American culture.
>
> All of us expect at least a minimum of obedience and conforming behavior from children. Most of us feel that a child who does not behave may deserve punishment. In spite of

initial horror and indignation expressed by people when they first hear of battered babies, most of those we talk with soon reveal how familiar they are with the feelings associated with such behavior.

The common denominator of our patients has been an adherence to a pattern of child rearing characterized by demand for premature high performance and satisfaction of parental needs. Accompanying this is complete disregard for what the infant might need and for his performance possibilities.

Specifically, parents — and I include anyone taking care of children — do not perceive the infant as an infant, but as an organized human being capable of sensing the parent's needs and meeting them. This phenomenon exists independently of variables such as socio-economic station, psychiatric diagnosis, age, sex, or relationship of the caretaker to the mistreated child.

In all our patients who have attacked children, we have seen a breakdown in "ability to mother." There is no great difference between men or women in this breakdown. By "mothering" we don't mean the superficial techniques of care, but the deep, sensitive, intuitive awareness of and response to the infant's condition and needs, as well as consideration of the infant's capacity to perform according to his age.

The parents are insensitive to the ebb and flow of the infant's needs. They are concentrating more on the needs they themselves have. This is role reversal in which parents act like a needy child and expect their child to take over the role of a satisfying parent.

This is a repetition of the parents' own childhood situation. They feel unloved, unlistened to, uncared for, and deeply worthless. We don't mean they didn't receive attention from their parents and families. On the contrary, they were often the focus of extreme concern which took the form of demand and attack rather than anything approximating kindness and sympathy. Their only sense of worth came when they were able to meet the exorbitant parental demands described, but this was rare and transient. Although this situation occurs at all levels of society, the type of performance demanded may be socio-economically determined.

The intensity of our patients' super-ego is striking. They are quite punitive and rigid. This shows up in psychological tests as well as in clinical data we obtain from them. . . .

When the child fails to perform in a way to make the parent feel good, the child becomes an evil environment, so to speak. Anger, resentment, and fury are aroused in the parent who then identifies the child with his own critical parent.

We have found that even though abusers feel their own parents were demanding and belittling of them, rarely have they faced their parents with this in reality.

As a rule, the child is not attacked on this identification basis alone. The abuser usually does not hit the child until he can rework the situation to see the child as his own bad, needy, crying self. Then the super-ego can approve the attack and punishment, because in this super-ego structure the parent has a right to attack a no-good infant. Repeatedly we hear parents say that hitting their baby was like hitting themselves.

Attacking parents look to other people for mothering besides their own mothers. Women look to husbands particularly, husbands look to wives. But if the mothering function fails in the environment, the parent quickly takes it out on the baby.

What provokes child beating? An incredible sense of aloneness, worthlessness, and strangely enough, desire — desire for the child to take care of the unheeded needs of the attacker's own yesterdays. When the baby cries or when the small child doesn't yield, his caretaker cannot tolerate the feeling provoked within himself. Attack is the only solution this caretaker knows.

Henry Makover of the Albert Einstein College of Medicine, a psychiatric consultant of the Family Court of New York, discussed at the workshop his observations and interpretations of child-abuse cases which come before the court and which may differ in certain respects from cases seen in hospitals and out-patient medical and psychiatric clinics. Excerpts from his discussion follow:

> The conditions that bring about the physical abuse of children often differ from those that result in neglect and deprivation in degree rather than in kind. This suggests the possibility of viewing the physically abused child as a special case of the deprived or neglected child.
> Physical damage to a child indicates more often than not a lack of impulse control which results in "acting out" aggression in a brutal and sometimes sadistic manner. . . .
> My observations indicate that overt mental illness, as manifested by psychotic or borderline behavior, is present more frequently in the parent or parents of the physically abused child than it is in the other forms of neglect. . . .
> Among the more overt forms of mental illness encountered in the parent or parents of abused children are: chronic paranoid schizophrenia, psychopathic personality, severe passive-aggressive character disorder, agitated depression, and particularly, the unresolved postpartum depression. Alcoholism, either accompanying some of the above conditions or as a presenting condition, is also seen, but more often as a precipitant due to its ability to inhibit the control of impulses. Narcotic addiction as a primary cause of physical abuse was infrequent though it certainly contributes to the neglect of

children by the squandering of the families' economic re-
serves. Certain forms of mental retardation can also serve as
an important contributing factor. Other forms of mental dis-
order, important clinically because of their often being more
difficult to diagnose, are sexual deviance, psycho-motor
equivalents, and unconscious displacement of anger at the
spouse or even at the parent's parents. . . . In the court
population, however, a high proportion of the families seen
show the effects of poverty and overcrowding, and, therefore, social stress is more likely to be present in these cases
on the basis of probability alone. Early marriage and parental immaturity, low educational level and unemployment,
may not be direct causes of the cruel behavior but they certainly do nothing to prevent it.

Since the parent or parents inflict the damage, we must, of
course, consider them as the prime subjects of investigation.
However, I have seen a few cases in which it would be difficult to deny the provocative behavior of the child as being
responsible for the event. Such children, themselves disturbed, may evoke severe parental punishment as a result of
psychotic or neurotic guilt. In fact, an emphasis on the interaction between parent and child would, perhaps, be the most
fruitful avenue of research.

Finally, in a very few cases, there may have been a mis-
taken attempt to solve a reality problem. The birth of an
unwanted child, either illegitimate or the last of too many,
may result in an attempted infanticide which is unsuccessful
and which results in remorse and a request for medical care.

The findings and interpretations of medical, psychiatric, and
social welfare investigators concerning physical abuse of children presented so far in this chapter were derived from observations on relatively small and unrepresentative study-samples in

specialized settings such as children's hospitals, courts, psychiatric clinics, and children's protective services. With the enactment of legislation concerning the reporting of physical abuse of children during the early sixties, a source for obtaining data on large numbers of abused children became available for the first time, and research began to shift from clinical studies toward large-scale surveys and epidemiologic studies. This shift resulted in certain advantages but also in shortcomings in terms of reliability and validity of research findings. The basis for sample selection was broadened considerably, yet samples of abused children derived through official reporting mechanisms are not necessarily free from systematic bias. Moreover, the detailed observations possible in clinical studies tend to be sacrificed in large-scale surveys and epidemiologic studies.

Some of the differences in findings and interpretations revealed in the foregoing review were clearly due to differences in the definitions used by various investigations as basis for sample selection. This particular difficulty continued to haunt designers of large-scale surveys and epidemiologic studies.

The first epidemiologic study of physical child abuse was conducted by the School of Public Health and Administrative Medicine of Columbia University under Drs. Simons and Downs. Summarizing their findings they state that

> Identification of abused children has assumed new significance with the passage of state laws requiring medical reporting of child abuse incidents. An epidemiologic study of 313 cases registered in New York City during the first year following the 1964 legislation demonstrated a broad spectrum of abuse patterns with a wide range of physical injuries. A strikingly high proportion of the reported children came from multiproblem families where the interplay of mental, physical, and environmental stresses could not be ignored as

etiologic factors, and where the abusive acts appeared chiefly as late indicators of serious family difficulties.[30]

Studies of officially reported cases of child abuse were conducted in several states following the enactment of reporting legislation, and some of these studies were eventually published.[31] Their findings revealed a different picture of families who abuse their children from the one that had emerged as a result of clinical case studies. This picture corresponds rather closely to findings of the Columbia University study and of the nationwide survey to be presented in subsequent chapters.

The literature concerning physical abuse of children has dealt not only with the etiology and the dynamics of this phenomenon and with the characteristics and circumstances of persons involved in abusive incidents, but also with legal, administrative, and treatment dimensions of the problem. Guidelines for legislation to regulate the reporting of child abuse, developed by the U.S. Children's Bureau[32] and the American Humane Association, respectively, have already been mentioned.[33] It has also been noted that these guidelines differed in their recommendations concerning the official agency to whom reports are to be made. The Children's Bureau recommended that reports be made to the police, since police authorities function in every community throughout the country, twenty-four hours a day. The Humane Association recommended public or private child-protective agencies as recipients of reports, since these agencies

30. Betty Simons et al., "Child Abuse — Epidemiologic Study of Medically Reported Cases," *New York State Journal of Medicine,* 66 (1966), 2783–2788.
31. State of Illinois, Department of Children and Family Services, *A Survey of the First Year — Illinois Child Abuse Act* (1966). Estelle Siker, "First Year's Experience in Connecticut with a Child Abuse Law," *Connecticut Health Bulletin,* 81 (1967), 53–59. State of Maryland, Department of Public Welfare, *Incidents of Suspected Child Abuse, January–June 1967, Research Report* No. 4 (1968).
32. See above, note 13.
33. See above, note 17.

were thought to be better qualified than police authorities to deal with child-abuse cases in a protective, nonpunitive, and therapeutic manner. It should be noted that both these guidelines failed to suggest specifically that fatal incidents be reported, and that medical examiners or coroners be required to report fatalities they suspect to be the result of physical abuse. This oversight was carried over into all the laws that were eventually enacted on the basis of the guidelines, with the exception of the laws passed by Arkansas, Hawaii, and Oregon.

As soon as the legislative guidelines of the Children's Bureau were published, they became the subject of controversy. The American Medical Association thought that the guidelines discriminated against physicians by singling them out as the only professional group responsible for reporting. The AMA was also concerned that parents would avoid bringing their children for medical care following an injury for fear of being suspected and reported. Furthermore, the AMA suggested that in addition to physicians, school personnel, social workers, and nurses should be required to report, since physicians tend to be the last professional group to see injured children. According to the AMA, reporting by social workers, teachers, and nurses could be more effective in bringing about early protective intervention. The views of the AMA were published in an editorial in the Association's *Journal* [34] and in a position statement accepted by its House of Delegates.[35] Subsequently, the AMA also developed its own legislative proposal, which leaves reporting to the discretion of physicians, nurses, teachers and social workers, rather than making it mandatory. Recipients of reports in the AMA proposal are child-welfare agencies *or* the police.

In 1965 the Council of State Governments published its model

34. "Battered Child Legislation," *Journal of American Medical Association,* 188 (1964), 386.
35. "Statement of Position on Protecting Children against Physical Abuse," adopted by AMA House of Delegates, June 24, 1964.

reporting law,[36] a compromise between the guidelines of the Children's Bureau and the American Humane Association. Finally, in 1966 the Committee on the Infant and Preschool Child of the American Academy of Pediatrics published its recommendations concerning the reporting of child-abuse incidents.[37] In contrast to the AMA recommendations, the Academy favored mandatory reporting by physicians to child welfare or police authorities. It also recommended the inclusion of a mandatory service clause in the law, and the establishment of central registries of reported incidents at the state level with provisions for the elimination of names of persons included in the registry for insufficient reasons. All the guidelines and legislative proposals recommended the granting of immunity from civil and criminal liability to persons making reports in good faith.

By the middle of 1967 all fifty states, Washington, D.C., and the Virgin Islands had enacted laws concerning the reporting of child abuse. In accordance with these laws, reporting is discretional in six states — Alaska, Missouri, New Mexico, North Carolina, Texas, and Washington. In all other states and territories reporting is mandatory. There are differences in the fifty-two laws concerning the age of a child up to which injuries are reportable, the conditions which are to be reported, the professional groups required to report, the official agencies to whom reports are to be made, the responsibilities and rights of persons making reports and of the official recipients of reports, the establishment of central registries, and penalties for failing to report under the law. These differences reflect not only different interests in the states but also the conflicting positions of the various groups who developed guidelines. Several comparative summaries of the various laws have been published since 1964.[38]

36. Council on State Governments, *Physical Abuse of Children: Suggested State Legislation* (1965).

37. "Maltreatment of Children — The Physically Abused Child," *Pediatrics,* 37 (1966), 377–382.

38. American Humane Association, *Review of Legislation to Protect*

Soon after the laws were enacted, in state after state it became clear that several problems limited the effectiveness of reporting as a measure toward prevention, treatment, and control. First, many physicians, especially those in private practice, continued to be either unaware of the provisions of the law or, though aware, hesitant to cooperate in implementing its provisions. As a result, reporting was erratic and tended to reflect different levels of interest and cooperation on the part of local medical practitioners and others, rather than the real incidence of child abuse.

Larry B. Silver, William Barton, and Christina C. Dublin of Children's Hospital in Washington, D.C. concluded on the basis of a survey of 450 physicians (half of whom responded) that "physicians are not sufficiently aware of the battered child syndrome or of community procedures for the management of cases of child abuse . . . One in five physicians reported rarely or never considering child abuse when seeing an injured child . . . one in six said they had failed to consider child abuse in a case that might have been child abuse . . . more than half the physicians said they did not know the correct procedure to follow in their community . . . almost one of every four physicians stated that he would not report a case of suspected battered child syndrome even if he were protected against legal action by the parents . . . the physician's main concern was that the evidence would not stand up in a court proceeding . . . other considerations that appear to inhibit the physician from reporting his suspicion of child abuse include difficulty on the part of the physician in accepting the reality of willful child abuse . . . and

---

the Battered Child (Denver, Col., 1964). Allan McCoid, "The Battered Child and Other Assaults upon the Family: Part One," *Minnesota Law Review,* 50 (1965), 1–58. Monrad G. Paulsen, "Legal Framework of Child Protection," *Columbia Law Review,* 66 (1966), 679–717. Paulsen, "Legal Protections against Child Abuse," *Children,* 13 (1966), 42–48. American Humane Association, *Child Abuse Legislation* (Denver, Col., 1966). Children's Bureau, *The Child Abuse Reporting Laws — A Tabular View* (Washington, D.C., 1966).

confusion over the meaning and scope of many basic terms describing child neglect and abuse." [39]

A second, perhaps even more serious, problem concerning the reporting of child-abuse incidents is the inadequacy of child welfare services in many communities throughout the country. The lack of adequate services for dealing constructively with the abused child, his siblings, and his parents once an incident is reported may turn reporting into a futile formality. Monrad G. Paulsen of the University of Virginia succinctly summarized the problem on the basis of his studies of legal protection against child abuse: "Reporting is, of course, not enough. After a report is made, something has to happen. A multidisciplinary network of protection needs to be developed in each community to implement the good intentions of the law. If child protective services are not available, reporters will no longer report. The promise of case-finding legislation, such as reporting laws, is that when a case is found, something is done about it. The legislatures which require reporting but do not provide the means for further protective action delude themselves and neglect children." [40]

A third problematic issue is that of "due process" for parents and children. The primary purpose of reporting legislation is the protection of the safety of children. Yet efforts to assure this safety may at times infringe upon the constitutional rights of parents, or of the children themselves. Kimberly B. Cheney of the School of Law at Yale University examined various aspects of this complicated issue in a recent paper:

The best way to assure both that due process of law is observed and that the values on which decisions are made are clearly stated is by providing parents with counsel if they

39. "Child Abuse Laws — Are They Enough?" *Journal of American Medical Association,* 199 (1967), 101–104.
40. Paulsen, "Legal Protections against Child Abuse," pp. 42–48.

cannot do so themselves, as New York does. Lawyers could help force those persons concerned with child [abuse and] neglect to grapple with the basic social and legal questions involved. Thus, a protective statute should make provision for counsel at the time of the court review, if requested, and clients should be informed of this right on the initial contact.

In summary, legal procedures are not impediments to swift correction of social ills. Observance of legal rights would help to ensure that protective decisions are based on the reasoned application of relevant criteria. This is more likely to protect children than striking at neglect with unknown values and uncertain policy." [41]

Cooperation between medical, welfare, and legal authorities, and efforts to improve mutual understanding of the different responsibilities assigned to them by society, is viewed by Cheney as the best chance for minimizing the inherent conflict between, on the one hand, an emphasis on the child's safety, and, on the other, an emphasis on due process and constitutional rights for the parent.

A final set of problems concerns the appropriateness of legal and administrative provisions of specific laws for constructive, protective intervention, and the feasibility of such intervention. Many psychiatrists and social workers prefer that reports not be made to law-enforcement agencies, since these agencies may symbolize a punitive rather than a helpful attitude by the community toward the parent. Silver, in a discussion of this issue addressed to physicians, summarized what may be called a therapeutic orientation:

The author feels that the best approach is a form of the social service approach in which the major goals are to pro-

41. "Safeguarding Legal Rights in Providing Protective Services," *Children,* 13 (1966), 86–92.

tect the child and to assist the family in making use of whatever community facilities it may need. After evaluating the parent or parents, appropriate action can be initiated. Some parents may need social or psychiatric help, some parents may need hospitalization, other parents may need criminal court action. Penalizing the parent or placing the parent in jail does not help the problem; in fact in many cases it may complicate the problem by depriving the family of the wage earner or by removing the mother, thus creating even greater disruption of family life and creating the need for a variety of community services, such as public assistance, foster home placement, homemaker services or other supportive measures. It is felt that the first task is to protect the child. Following this the major emphasis should be on helping to minimize the family or intra-psychic stress which created the battering need. By offering help and not prosecution, the parents will be more available to look at the family difficulties and to accept community assistance in coping with the difficulties.[42]

The orientation reflected in the foregoing excerpt assumes that abusing parents are sick people in need of treatment and help, and that social workers, psychiatrists, and other therapists have the knowledge to treat and cure their sickness. Both these assumptions have been questioned by some investigators and writers. As for the first, it has been pointed out that not all incidents of abuse have a single set of etiological factors, and, consequently, while some abusive parents may indeed be sick, others may be quite normal and may merely follow a culturally acceptable child-rearing pattern, perhaps in a somewhat exaggerated manner because of situational stress. Concerning the

42. Larry B. Silver, "Child Abuse Syndrome: A Review," *Medical Times,* 96 (1968), 803–818.

second assumption, it has been suggested that to the extent that abusive parents are sick, their personality deviations are of a type that is resistant to known methods of treatment, and social workers, psychiatrists, and other therapists have had only limited success with cases of this type. Norman Polansky, himself an experienced therapist, social scientist, and researcher at the University of Georgia, in a recent report to the Joint Commission on Mental Health for Children questioned the ability of therapists to achieve personality change in abusive parents which would assure the welfare of the children.[43] His skepticism led him to view physical abuse of children as "an area in which social, medical, and legal action must be authoritative, intrusive and insistent." His views are summarized in his recommendations to the Joint Commission on Mental Health for Children:

> Our ignorance regarding the problems of child abuse and child neglect is, in the year 1968, not quite total, but it is severe enough to be inexcusable. We do not know what the incidence nor prevalence of these conditions are. We do not know how to go about casefinding and/or identification of these conditions. We have little knowledge of how to discriminate levels of severity, and are poor at prognosticating future course, with or without available treatments, in many instances. Finally, we do not know how to "treat" either of these social conditions in the sense of bringing about enduring change in the parents involved with much consistency, and with any efficiency. Other than that, we are scientifically in an excellent position.
>
> Based upon the little that *is* known, however, it is evident that:
>
> a. Child neglect and child abuse are distinguishable pa-

43. Norman and Nancy Polansky, "The Current Status on Child Abuse and Child Neglect in This Country," Report to the Joint Commission on Mental Health for Children (February 1968).

rental patterns, theoretically and empirically, although they are occasionally coincidental.

b. The child is in the greatest danger from both abuse and severe neglect below the age of three. He is often in noteworthy danger of death; minimally, he will be marked for life by events having irreversible sequellae in his emotional adjustment, and in his ability to learn and earn his living.

c. The degree of danger to the child is customarily under-, rather than overestimated by the public in general. This is reflected in judgments made by public prosecutors and judges in the handling of such cases as do eventually come to court.

d. Because of their dedication to the notion of "the family," or their zeal about "rehabilitation," the formal policies of social agencies in this field are sanguine to the point of being fatuous regarding the potentiality for change in a large proportion of the parents involved. The fact is that most hard-headed observers report *little success* with the methods of aggressive casework (or unaggressive psychiatry) now being practiced. This is true even when an adequate attempt at treatment is made, something which is possible in only a few areas of the country. The state of the art, in 1968 in the richest nation in history, is poor, even as compared with England and Holland.

It is because of these conclusions that we have made the following recommendations, some of which may seem rather shocking to people accustomed to viewing with genial detachment the sufferings of children outside their own families.

1. Wherever there is either clear evidence, or even persuasive evidence, of abuse of a child under the age of three, he should be permanently removed from the pa-

rental home. Return to the original parental home should be regarded as the rare exception, rather than the hoped-for norm.

2. Whenever a child is removed from a family because of evidence of "battering," or sexual abuse, etc. the non-guilty parent should be placed on probation, and forbidden to remove any other children they have from the possibility of continuous and intensive surveillance by the court of jurisdiction. Surveillance by a social agency is unlikely to be useful, since there is little in the training or experience or personal weaponry of a social worker likely to make her able to carry out this role effectively. We recommend that this be regarded as a police department or sheriff's function.

3. The parent found responsible for child battering should be held guilty of a felony, of course. This should be punishable by a substantial term in prison, for this parent, rather than probation. This is because of the known instances in which a parent, fixed in this pattern, has still murdered his child even while supposedly on probation — a typically loosely-administered gesture at this stage of our national development.

4. Children neglected to the point of starvation or actual abandonment by their parents should be promptly removed from the home, with the expectation that they will not be returned for a considerable period of time. Reconstitution of the family, if it is attempted, should be undertaken cautiously, and the assumption should be that change in the parents is a process which will require a number of years, rather than a few months.

5. The "failure to thrive" syndrome has been reasonably well-established and the findings regarding those cases in which its source lies within the mother's psychologi-

cal make-up should be made general knowledge among the relevant medical and social agency personnel. Specifically, pediatricians, obstetricians and general practitioners should be alerted to the nature of the psychological pattern, as should nursing personnel in the hospital setting. The law should require that when this is the diagnosis made, the child must be returned for regular check-ups at a suitable and reputable clinic. This is to counter the tendency of these mothers to defend against recognizing the problem by "doctor-shopping," etc. Such children should be treated, legally, like persons protected for their own good against failure to treat venereal disease, tuberculosis, or the like.

6. The correlation between a low level of child care and large family size is unmistakable, regardless of the cultural or presumed religious backgrounds of those involved. For many couples of low intelligence, or otherwise psychologically inadequate, the provision of birth control information is inadequate to prevent the *intergenerational treadmill*. It is recommended that the excellent laws in North Carolina regarding *sterilization* be adopted by the other states as constituting the most effective, if late, preventative they can make available. That is, sterilization should be available to any married person who wants it, with the consent of the marital partner. Sterilization operations should be made available free to those unable to pay, with the county bearing the cost. We have seen improvement in some women following this operation, alone!

7. In view of the evidence before us, it should become a general legal principle that no woman should have to bear a child whom she really does not want, providing she is capable of making such a choice. This applies to the law regarding abortion, and its availability to low-

income women, or those unable to manipulate an abortion under the current laws. . . .

Polansky's views concerning the potential effectiveness of therapeutic intervention with respect to reported cases of child abuse differ markedly from those expressed by Drs. Steele and Pollock of the University of Colorado School of Medicine. These two psychiatrists are optimistic concerning the potential of psychiatric and social work therapy to modify the child-rearing patterns of abusive parents, provided such parents are treated in an accepting, nonpunitive manner that meets their own needs for a satisfying and rewarding experience as parents, an experience they have never known in relation to their own parents. These views are reflected in the following excerpt from a recent book:

Our treatment of those who abuse infants has been directed toward improving the basic pattern of child rearing. It is based upon the hypotheses derived from the study of the psychology of abusing parents in our group. We were able to establish useful contact with all but a few of the sixty families, and of this treated group well over three-fourths showed significant improvement. Some changed a great deal, some only moderately, some are still in therapy. We considered it improvement when dangerously severe physical attack of the infant was eliminated and milder physical attack in the form of a disciplinary punishment was either eliminated or reduced to non-injurious minimum. Of equal significance was a reduction in demand upon and criticism of children accompanied by increased recognition of a child as an individual with age appropriate needs and behavior. Further, signs of improvement in the parents were increased abilities to relate to a wider social milieu for pleasurable satisfaction and source of help in time of need rather than looking to their children for such responses. We did not always try nor did we always succeed in making any change in all of the psychological conflicts and character problems of our patients. These were dealt with only as the patient wished or as far as we thought necessary in relation to our primary therapeutic goal. Our philosophy of the value of treatment is twofold; first, it deals in the most humanitarian and constructive way we know with a tragic facet of people's lives; second, therapeutic intervention in a process which seems to pass from one generation to the next will hopefully produce changes in patterns of child rearing toward the lessening of unhappiness and tragedy.[44]

The foregoing review of the work of researchers and professionals in the field suggests that progress has been achieved during recent decades toward a better understanding of child abuse and its etiology and also in society's ability to deal with this problem. At the same time, few questions concerning the dynamics of child abuse and appropriate societal responses to it were answered satisfactorily. Disagreement among scholars and professionals continues to exist with regard to nearly every aspect of this phenomenon — its scope, its nature, and measures for dealing with it.

44. Brandt F. Steele and Carl B. Pollock, "A Psychiatric Study of Parents Who Abuse Infants and Small Children," in Helfer and Kempe, *The Battered Child,* pp. 103–147.

Chapter Three

Opinions and Attitudes

Nowhere in the extensive literature is there any systematic reference to what knowledge, attitudes, and opinions Americans have about physical abuse of children. And yet, the social and cultural context of this phenomenon cannot be fully comprehended unless these attitudes and opinions are unraveled. A survey of public awareness, attitudes, and opinions concerning child abuse in the United States was conducted as a first step in the present program of studies. The survey was administered during October 1965 by the National Opinion Research Center (NORC) of the University of Chicago. In addition to explaining prevailing attitudes concerning physical child abuse in America, the survey was also designed to obtain an indirect estimate of the scope of this phenomenon within the United States.

For purposes of this survey child abuse was defined operationally as an occurrence in which a caretaker, usually an adult, injures a child, not by accident, but in anger or deliberately.

More specifically, "child abuse" was defined in the interview schedule in the following manner:

> Now some questions about child abuse. I want to make clear exactly what I mean. Child abuse is when an adult physically injures a child, not by accident, but in anger or deliberately. Sometimes the person injuring the child is a parent, older brother or sister, or other relative. It could also be a baby-sitter, a teacher, or someone else who is not related to the child — but it would *always* be someone who is at least temporarily taking care of the child.

As can be seen, the operational definition used in the survey included only incidents of child abuse which resulted in physical injury of some kind. It excluded abusive physical attacks which did not result in physical injury but which are, nevertheless, part of the phenomenon in accordance with the conceptual definition presented in Chapter I, above.

Method of the Survey

The survey employed a standard national multistage area probability sample of the total noninstitutional population of the United States, 21 years old or older, to the block or segment level. Married respondents under 21 years old were considered a part of this population and, accordingly, interviewed whenever encountered in the quota sampling. At the block level, respondents were selected according to quotas of sex, age, race, and employment status. This quota sample, consisting of 1,520 respondents, had about the same efficiency as a simple random sample of 1,000 respondents. The standard error of proportions for such a sample does not exceed 1.6 percent.[1] Percentages

1. National Opinion Research Center, *The Sample Design for NORC's Amalgam Surveys,* mimeographed, issued by NORC, University of Chicago (no date), p. 4.

quoted in the following discussion, therefore, may be extrapolated to the universe of about 110 million adults in the United States within the stated margin of error, and with 95 percent confidence.

The survey concerning attitudes on child abuse was administered as part of an "amalgam-survey." This means that the survey interview focused on several different topics of which child abuse was only one. Background information on the respondents themselves was also gathered during the interview.[2]

The following issues were explored by the survey in the section dealing with child abuse. First, public knowledge and opinions about the general problem of child abuse was ascertained. Had anything been heard or read during the preceding year or ever? What were the sources of knowledge? What should be done with children abused by their caretakers? What should be done with the perpetrators of child abuse? Which agency should have primary responsibility for dealing with the whole problem of child abuse? What did the respondents think they would do if they learned about a child being abused in the neighborhood? What did the respondents think they would do if they happened to be present while a child was being abused?

The survey also investigated awareness of specific incidents of child abuse during the preceding year, the sources of knowledge, and whether respondents personally knew the families involved. By virtue of the nationally representative character of the sample, the latter piece of information seemed especially important for obtaining an estimate of the upper bound of yearly incidence of child abuse in the United States. The background characteristics, circumstances, and dispositions of the child and the perpetrator were obtained for incidents involving families of which the respondents had personal knowledge.

Knowledge of community resources and their use was another

2. Copies of questionnaires used in the survey can be obtained from the author.

focus of study. Respondents were asked if they had ever heard about any educational programs or activities dealing with child abuse. What organizations sponsored them? Did they ever attend or participate in any of them? Did they know of any agencies which could be called upon specifically to protect children abused by their caretakers?

An attempt was also made to assess how widespread the propensity to child abuse might be in the general population. A series of interrelated questions funneled the issue down to the individual respondent. Did the respondent think that anybody is capable of child abuse? Did he think that he might himself injure a child in his care someday? Was there ever a time when he could hardly refrain from abusing a child? Did he ever actually lose control and injure a child in his care?

Finally, the respondents were asked how much publicity child abuse should receive.

In analyzing the total response to the survey the investigators attempted to learn whether the respondents' marital status, parenthood, work status, education, religion, age, income, sex, race, and place of residence, singly or interacting, influenced their responses to the various questions.

A special computer program designed to select optimal combinations of explanatory variables was used in the analysis.[3] Taking into account all the possible combinations of a set of independent variables and values on them, the program employs a nonsymmetric branching process, based on variance analytic techniques, to divide a sample into the series of subgroups which maximizes prediction of values on specified dependent variables. The assumptions of linearity and additivity required in conventional multiple regression analysis are not necessary here. The dependent variable, however, must be a continuous or equal-interval

3. John A. Sonquist and James N. Morgan, *The Detection of Interaction Effects: A Report on a Computer Program for the Selection of Optimal Combinations of Explanatory Variables,* Monograph 35 (Ann Arbor, Survey Research Center, University of Michigan, 1964).

scale. Dichotomies are permissible as minimal equal-interval scales. In the approach to the analytic task with help of the Automatic Interaction Detector the usual question, "What is the effect of x on y when everything else is held constant?" is replaced with the more comprehensive question: What configurations of values of independent variables are associated with specified values of dependent variables?" The latter question seems more appropriate than the former when theory is not precise about the relationships between variables and when exact hypotheses are not being tested. This is often the situation in survey research.

Characteristics of Respondents to Survey

The 1520 respondents were 48.5 percent male and 51.5 percent female. They were 85.7 percent white, 13.4 percent Negro, .3 percent Oriental, and .7 percent other races. About 69 percent were Protestant, 25.9 percent Roman Catholic, 2 percent Jewish, and 0.8 percent other; 2.8 percent had no religious preference. With respect to age, about 11 percent were under 25; 45.9 percent, between 26 and 45; 16.5 percent, between 46 and 55; 12.7 percent, between 56 and 65; and 14.3 percent, over 65. Fewer than .3 percent of the respondents had no formal education. Twenty-two percent had attended school eight years or less; 21.1 percent, some high school; 43.7 percent, high school and some college; 6.5 percent, college; and 6.5 percent, graduate or professional school.

About 81 percent of the respondents were married at the time of the survey; 7.7 percent, widowed; 2.8 percent, divorced; 1.7 percent, separated; and 7.2 percent, single, never married. Roughly 12 percent of the married respondents had no children. Of those who had children, 73.8 percent had from 1 to 4; 11.9 percent, from 5 to 7; and 2 percent, 8 or more.

Fifty-one percent of the respondents were working full or part-time; 3.1 percent were temporarily out of work because of illness, vacation, strike, etc.; 1.1 percent, unemployed, looking for work; 10.9 percent, retired; 31.7 percent, at home keeping house; and 1.6 percent, in school or otherwise occupied. About 15 percent of the respondents who had ever worked were professional or technical workers; 4.9 percent, owners or managers of farms or ranches; 8 percent, managers, officials or proprietors; 19.1 percent, clerical workers; 6.3 percent, sales workers; 13.3 percent, craftsmen and foremen; 15.9 percent, machine operators; 12.6 percent, service workers occupied outside of households; and 4.6 percent, laborers, There were no farm or mine laborers and foremen in the sample.

Gross family income ranged from under $2,000 to over $15,000. About 11 percent of the respondents had gross family incomes of under $2,000; 18.6 percent, from $2,000 to $3,999; 20.2 percent, from $4,000 to $5,999; 19 percent, from $6,000 to $7,999; 11.2 percent, from $8,000 to $9,999; 13.5 percent, from $10,000 to $14,999; and 6.2 percent, $15,000 or more.

Forty-one percent of the respondents lived in "smaller" metropolitan areas; 24.3 percent, in major metropolitan areas; 15.9 percent, in counties with a town of 10,000 to 49,999 population; and 18.7 percent, in counties with no town of 10,000.[4] Their distribution over the nine geographic areas of the United States defined by the U.S. Census Bureau approximated the percentages projected for 1965.

Interviewers rated 83.9 percent of the respondents very cooperative when interviewed; 15.1 percent, somewhat cooperative; and 1.1 percent, noncooperative. Fifty-eight percent were

4. For sampling purposes NORC refined the U.S. Census Bureau definition of the Standard Metropolitan Statistical Area. Under the refinement, a major metropolitan area consists of an SMSA with a total population of 2 million or more. A smaller metropolitan area consists of an SMSA with less than 2 million total population. See U.S. Census Bureau, *County and City Data Book, 1967* (Washington, D.C., Government Printing Office, 1967), pp. xiii–xiv, for the official definition.

rated very interested in the topics about which they were questioned; 38.5 percent, somewhat interested; and 3.5 percent, uninterested.

Propensity to Child Abuse

Perhaps the most important issue explored in the survey was the propensity in the population to inflict physical injury upon a child. This was explored by means of a set of questions that funneled the issue down to the individual respondent. To assure fullest possible comprehension of the meaning of this set of questions on the part of respondents the following wording was used:

— "I will just repeat once more what I mean by *child-abuse* — that is when an adult physically injures a child in his care, either deliberately or because he lost his temper. Do you think that almost anyone could at some time injure a child in his care?"

— "Do you think that you yourself might possibly injure a child at some time?"

— "Was there ever a time when you could hardly keep yourself from injuring a child in your care?"

— "Did you ever actually lose control of yourself and injure a child?"

Table I shows the opinions of respondents in reply to the first of this series of questions.

As shown in Table I nearly six out of every ten respondents to the survey, or of the adult U.S. population to which these findings can be extrapolated, thought that anybody could at some time injure a child in his care. This large proportion seems to suggest that the infliction of physical injury upon children is viewed as an "almost normal occurrence" in the course of caring for a child. It should be noted again that physical abuse, for pur-

Table 1. Respondents' Opinion on the Propensity to Child Abuse in the Population at Large

Opinion	Number	Percentage
"Almost anybody could at some time injure a child in his care"	884	58.3
"Not everybody is capable of injuring a child in his care"	592	39.1
Did not know	40	2.6
Total	1516[a]	100.0

[a] Excluding 4 respondents who did not answer.

poses of this survey, included only incidents resulting in physical injury inflicted by a caretaker and excluded physical attacks which did not result in injury. If the definition used included also physical attack that did not result in injury, it is likely that an even higher proportion of the respondents would have expressed the opinion that almost anybody could at some time abuse a child in his care.

As can be expected, when the question of propensity was focused directly on the respondent rather than on the population at large, a drop in estimates took place, as shown in Tables 2 and 3.

Table 2. Respondents' Opinion on Their Own Propensity to Child Abuse

Opinion	Number	Percentage
Respondent thought he could at some time injure a child	338	22.3
Respondent thought he could never injure a child	1141	75.2
Did not know	39	2.6
Total	1518[a]	100.0

[a] Excluding 2 respondents who did not answer.

Table 3. Respondents' Admission of Capacity for Child Abuse

Group	Number of Respondents in Group	Percentage of Group Admitting Capacity
55 years of age or under, male	508	34.0
55 years of age or under, female	599	20.0
Over 55 years of age, both sexes	413	12.0
All groups together	1520	22.3

Thus, while only 22.3 percent of the entire sample considered themselves "at risk" to physically injure a child some time, 34 percent of men under age 55, as against 20 percent of women in this age group, considered themselves at such a risk. Among respondents of either sex over 55 years of age, the self-classification of being subject to such a risk drops off to 12 percent, which, too, is not a negligible portion.

Respondents were next asked how close they had actually come to abusing a child. The results are shown in Table 4.

Table 4. How Close Respondents Came to Child Abuse

Proximity to Abusing Child	Number	Percentage
Respondent at one time could hardly refrain from injuring a child in his care	242	15.9
Respondent never came close to injuring a child in his care	1276	84.1
Total	1518[a]	100.0

[a] Excluding 2 respondents who did not answer.

Considering the fact that an admission of having come very close to injuring a child in one's care may not be easy to make to a stranger in a survey of this kind, the 15.9 percent of the respondents who did make such an admission are likely to represent a low estimate, and the true proportion of adults in the U.S.

population who come very close to injuring a child physically is likely to be higher.

The final question in this series, the admission of having physically injured a child in one's care some time in the past, was answered affirmatively by 6 respondents, 0.4 percent of the sample. This figure, too, is likely to represent the lowest possible estimate, since it actually involves the admission of an illegal act.

The findings reported here concerning propensity to child abuse seem to support the theoretical premise according to which a certain measure of physical abuse of children tends to be condoned by American culture as a "normal" aspect of rearing children. For otherwise it would not be likely for such large proportions of the adult population to respond positively to the items exploring the general and their own propensity to child abuse.

The Upper Limit of Incidence

One item in the survey was designed to provide an indirect, rough estimate of the upper limit of the annual incidence of child abuse in the United States population. Respondents were asked whether they personally knew families involved in incidents of child abuse resulting in physical injury during the twelve months preceding the interview. Forty-five, or 3 percent of the 1520 respondents, reported such personal knowledge of 48 different incidents in the course of one year. The comprehension of respondents of the definition of child abuse as used in the survey was tested in the interview by means of a supplementary questionnaire that required detailed description and actual identification of each child-abuse incident of which they claimed personal knowledge during the preceding year. In this way the attempt was made to ascertain that all incidents reported in response to this question did indeed occur, and fit the definition used in the survey.

At the time of the survey there were about 110 million adults, 21 years of age and over in the United States, who constituted the universe sampled by the survey. Sample proportions obtained in the survey may be extrapolated to this universe within a known margin of error, which in the case of 3 percent, at the 95 percent level of confidence, is less than 0.7 percent. Accordingly, it is possible to state that 2.3 percent to 3.7 percent of 110 million adults, or 2.53 to 4.07 million adults throughout the United States, knew personally families involved in incidents of child abuse during the year preceding the October 1965 survey.

If each of these adults knew a different family involved in abusing and injuring a child, the number of families abusing children during the year preceding the survey would equal the number of adults having personal knowledge of such families. In that unlikely case the figures 2.53 and 4.07 millions, respectively, would represent, with 95 percent certainty, the lower and upper limits of the annual, nationwide incidence of child abuse resulting in some injury known outside the home of abused children. It must be remembered in this context that some incidents of child abuse are completely unknown beyond the confines of the abused child's home. Information concerning such completely invisible incidents was not expected to be revealed by means of a survey of the type discussed here.

The actual incidence rate of child abuse known outside the abused child's home is, however, likely to be lower than suggested by the foregoing discussion, since some of the 2.53 to 4.07 million adults who according to this estimate personally knew families involved in child-abuse incidents are likely to have known the same family. Data from the survey do not permit an estimate of the proportion of incidents known to more than one person. As far as could be ascertained, there were no multiple known cases at all among those known to the respondents of the survey. Common sense suggests, however, that some of the families involved in abusing children are likely to be known personally to more than one person, and therefore the total number of families known to have abused children is likely to be considerably smaller than the total number of individuals having personal knowledge of such families. Accordingly, the survey provided only an estimate of the *upper limit* in the total United States population of the incidence of child abuse resulting in injury from minimal to fatal, and known beyond the confines of the abused child's home. This upper limit for the year ending October 1965 was between 2.53 and 4.07 million for a population of about 190 million, or about 13.3 to 21.4 incidents per 1000 persons. The actual incidence rate, however, was not determined by the survey and is likely to be considerably lower.

It should be noted once more that this estimate of the upper limit of the annual incidence of child abuse is very rough, having been obtained by means of an indirect method, the reliability and validity of which are unknown.

Knowledge of the Problem

About 80 percent of the respondents to the survey had heard or read about the general problem of child abuse and about specific incidents during the year preceding the survey, and an additional 12 percent had heard about this issue prior to that year. Education, place of residence, and parental status influenced knowledgeability. Respondents who were parents, had higher education, and were living in metropolitan areas were most likely to be aware of the problem. Taking into account all who had ever heard or read about child abuse, one can conclude that very few people in the United States are unaware of the general problem.

As can be seen from Table 5, most respondents learned about child abuse through the mass media of communication, while professional personnel and various social institutions accounted only for a small percentage of the sources of information. This

Table 5. Source of Respondents' Knowledge of the General Problem
of Child Abuse during the Year Preceding the Survey

Source	Number[a]	Percent of Total Sample (1520 Respondents)
Newspapers	1094	72.0
Radio, television	854	56.2
Magazines	345	22.7
Conversation with friends, neighbors, colleagues, or others	320	21.0
Doctors, nurses, or other medical personnel in a hospital or medical office	79	5.2
Churches or synagogues	58	3.8
Teachers or other school personnel, or PTA	52	3.4
Clubs or organizations	37	2.4
Professional associations	36	2.4
Others	31	2.0

[a] This column does not add up to 1520, since many respondents
mentioned more than one source.

latter fact seems to be of considerable importance in planning
preventive measures.

Knowledge of Child Protective Agencies

While knowledge of the phenomenon of child abuse was widespread throughout the population, the knowledge about agencies
in the community to whom one could turn for help in connection
with incidents of abuse was more limited. Table 6 shows the
level of this knowledge in various subgroups and in the entire
sample. Place of residence and education interacted to influence
knowledgeability. Residents of major metropolitan areas, irrespective of educational status, were least knowledgeable, while
respondents who lived outside major metropolitan areas, and

Chapter Three

Table 6. Respondents' Knowledge of Child Protective Agencies in the Community

Group	Number of Respondents in Group	Percentage of Group Who Had Knowledge
Nonmajor metropolitan areas, above high school education	303	66.0
Nonmajor metropolitan areas, high school or less education	848	50.0
Major metropolitan areas, all levels of education	369	38.0
All groups together	1520	50.4

had higher education, were most knowledgeable. It thus seems that residents of areas with heavy population concentration, who are likely to have greater need for protective services, are least knowledgeable about such services.

Reactions to Child Abuse

Two items in the survey explored how respondents thought they would react should an incident of child abuse occur in their neighborhood, or should they happen to be actually present at such an incident. Answers to these items are shown in Tables 7 and 8 respectively.

Additional analysis of the data in Table 7 suggests that race and education somewhat influenced how respondents thought they would react to child-abuse incidents in their neighborhood.

Among the nonwhite respondents 32 percent said they would attempt to talk personally with the family of the abused child, while only 11 percent of white respondents indicated readiness for such direct self-involvement. This difference seems to suggest that nonwhite neighborhoods may be more cohesive than white neighborhoods and may also prefer to exclude outsiders from their affairs. It also may reflect the nonwhite community's distrust of white dominated welfare agencies and police departments.

Table 7. How Respondents Thought They Would React upon Learning
That a Child in the Neighborhood Had Been Abused

Reaction	Number	Percentage
Would talk directly with the child's family	207	13.7
Would discuss it with neighbors to decide what steps to take	132	8.7
Would not get involved with family or neighbors but would notify police	357	23.6
Would not get involved with family or neighbors but would notify local welfare agency	690	45.6
Would keep out of it, having no business mixing in other people's affairs	107	7.1
Did not know	19	1.3
Total	1512[a]	100.0

[a] Excluding 8 respondents who did not answer.

Table 8. How Respondents Thought They Would React if Present
While a Child Was Being Abused

Reaction	Number	Percentage
Would try to stop person somehow and protect child from being injured	1157	76.7
Would not interfere but would call police	181	12.0
Would not interfere but would call local welfare agency	115	7.6
Would keep out of it, having no business mixing in other people's affairs	42	2.8
Did not know	14	.9
Total	1509[a]	100.0

[a] Excluding 11 respondents who did not answer.

Among respondents with at least a high school education,
52 percent indicated that they would contact a welfare agency
if they learned of a child-abuse incident in their neighborhood,
while only 37 percent of respondents with less than a high
school education intended to contact a welfare agency.

It is also interesting to note that only 7 percent of all respondents indicated that they would take no action at all and would not mix in their neighbors' affairs, if they heard of an incident of child abuse.

Although the data in Table 7 suggest that, on the whole, respondents seem to be quite reluctant to become personally involved with the family of an abused child upon a hearsay report of a child-abuse incident in the neighborhood, the contingency of witnessed child abuse evoked a very different response. As can be seen in Table 8, 76.7 percent of the respondents thought they would try somehow to stop the abuse and to protect the child from his attacker. Roughly 20 percent would not interfere by themselves but would call the police or a welfare agency for help, and only about 3 percent of the respondents thought they would not become involved in any way. Further analysis revealed that 79 percent of respondents under 65 years of age thought they would try to stop the perpetrator if present while a child was being abused. Sixty percent of respondents over 65 years old thought they would intervene in a like manner. This does reflect the realistic constraint that age has upon people getting into a fracas over any issue. That 60 percent of the respondents over 65 years old would risk possible physical injury in coming to the rescue of a child they saw being abused is itself noteworthy.

It is important to keep in mind that the responses reported in Tables 7 and 8 reflect verbalized attitudes and not actual behavior. Since verbalized attitudes tend to be influenced by dominant social values to a higher degree than actual behavior, one must be cautious in translating the stated reactions of the respondents into conclusions about what they would actually do when learning of a case of child abuse in their neighborhood or when witnessing an actual incident.

Treatment of the Child and Perpetrators

The opinions respondents held concerning appropriate measures for the protection of physically abused children and concerning appropriate ways of dealing with the perpetrators of child abuse are shown in Tables 9 and 10. These tables indicate that the

Table 9. What Respondents Thought Should Be Done about an Abused Child

Disposition	Number	Percentage
Child should be removed from care of person who caused injury the first time incident happens	535	36.0
Child should be removed from home only as last resort. Parent or other caring for child should be given "second chance" and should be supervised and helped to improve care of child	801	53.9
If it seems unlikely that person who injured child would do it again, it's OK to leave child in his or her care	119	8.0
None of these	20	1.3
Did not know	10	.7
Total	1485[a]	100.0

[a] Excluding 35 respondents who did not answer.

majority of the respondents seem to have a tolerant and understanding attitude toward the abusing parent, an attitude not always shared by professionals and officials dealing with child abuse. It seems that the tolerant attitude expressed by the majority of the respondents may reflect the cultural approval of a certain measure of physical abuse of children by caretakers.

The educational level and the sex of the respondents influenced their opinions concerning appropriate measures for dealing with the abused child. Fifty-two percent of females with less than high school education favored the removal of an abused child

Table 10. What Respondents Thought Should Be Done about Perpetrators of Child Abuse

Disposition	Number	Percentage
Such parents or other persons should be jailed or punished in some other way	409	27.1
Such parents or other persons must be closely supervised and treated rather than punished	1003	66.4
Such parents or other persons should be left alone if the injury is not too serious	66	4.4
None of these	22	1.5
Did not know	11	.7
Total	1511[a]	100.0

[a] Excluding 9 respondents who did not answer.

from the care of the person who injured him, the first time such an incident occurred. Only 36 percent of the males at the same educational level favored such a radical course, indicating that males may show more tolerance toward parents who use physical force against their children. Only 30 percent of either sex with high school education or more favored the radical approach of removing the child from the custody of the perpetrator after a first incident. Education thus seems to strengthen tolerance. The influence of education in the direction of tolerance is revealed also by the respondents' opinions on dealing with the perpetrators. While 66.4 percent of all respondents opposed punishment of perpetrators and suggested they be supervised and treated, 76 percent of respondents with a high school education or more favored such a tolerant approach toward perpetrators, as against 54 percent of respondents with less than a high school education.

The predominantly tolerant attitude of respondents concerning the phenomenon of child abuse was further illustrated in their opinions as to which community agency should assume primary responsibility for handling child-abuse cases. Social welfare and health agencies were favored by 69 percent of the respondents, while law enforcement agencies were favored by 22.7 percent. Six percent thought responsibility should reside in one or more combinations of these agencies, and about 2 percent either suggested some other type of agency or had no opinion.

Educational Programs and Activities

Most people in the United States were not aware of the various educational programs and activities dealing with child abuse in their community. Only 21.3 percent of the respondents were aware of them.

Table 11. Types of Educational Programs or Activities Dealing with Child Abuse of Which Respondents Were Aware

Type	Number of Respondents	Percent of Total Sample[a]
Did not know	84	5.5
TV	80	5.3
Social service agency	62	4.1
School, PTA	46	3.0
Church, synagogue	39	2.6
Hospital, clinic, medical organization	33	2.2
Mental health clinic, child guidance clinic	32	2.1
Other sources	27	1.8
Professional organization	18	1.2
Club or organization	15	1.0
Neighborhood center, settlement house, YMCA	8	.5
Labor union	2	.1

[a] 1520 respondents.

Table 11 indicates the types of programs and activities of which the respondents were aware. Some respondents knew of more than one type. Five and one-half percent of the respondents knew of programs and activities but could not specify the type.

Only 3.2 percent of the respondents had ever participated in programs and activities dealing with child abuse. If sponsors of educational programs and activities dealing with child abuse were aiming at a broad segment of the population, one can conclude that their efforts have been about 20 percent effective as far as gaining recognition for their efforts is concerned, but only 3.2 percent effective as far as participation is concerned. However, some programs on radio and TV may have an educational impact not apparent to listeners and viewers. Whereas 56.2 percent of the respondents cited radio and TV as the source of their knowledge about the general problem of child abuse, only 5.3 percent identified TV as the type of educational program to which they had been exposed. On the other hand, the percentages specifying other types of educational programs and activities and other sources of information about the general problem of child abuse are more nearly compatible.

Publicity

Respondents were asked how much publicity they thought child abuse should receive. On the assumption that response to this question may provide an indication of the extent of concern with this problem, it seems that 30.1 percent of the population at the time of the survey was very concerned. They thought child abuse should receive a lot of publicity. Another 44 percent thought it should receive some publicity — an indication of moderate concern. Roughly 22 percent, on the other hand, thought the subject should be kept quiet. About 4 percent could offer no opinion.

Seventy-nine percent of the respondents 45 years old or younger favored giving child abuse at least some publicity in contrast to 68 percent of the respondents over 45 years old.

Summary

In summarizing this survey of public knowledge, attitudes, and opinion about physical child abuse in the United States the following points may be made:

Most American adults are aware of the existence of the phenomenon of child abuse, mainly through the mass media of communication. Only one half of the population knows of specific agencies to which it can turn to request protection for an abused child, and only about one fifth is aware of various educational programs concerning the problem of child abuse.

About 3 percent of American adults have personal knowledge in the course of a year of families who abused and physically injured a child. This suggests a maximum annual incidence rate of physical injury due to child abuse of approximately 2.53 to 4.07 millions. The actual maximum figure is likely to be lower, and it should be noted that this figure includes all kinds of injury from minimal through serious to fatal. It should also be noted that this is an indirect and very rough estimate, obtained by means of a method the reliability and validity of which are unknown.

Six out of ten American adults think that almost anyone could at some time physically abuse a child in his care. The majority of Americans also show a rather tolerant attitude toward perpetrators of abuse, favoring treatment and supervision for them, and rejecting punishment. They think social welfare and health agencies, rather than law enforcement agencies, should carry primary responsibility for dealing with the problem of child abuse, and that abused children should be removed from the care of abusive parents only as a last resort.

A large majority of American adults indicate readiness to personally intervene and protect a child, should they happen to be present when a child was abused physically. The majority also think they would take steps for the protection of an abused child should they learn of an incident of abuse in their neighborhood. Such steps would involve reporting to a social agency or to the police but not direct intervention with the child's family. Only a minority would approach directly an abusive family in their neighborhood.

Chapter Four

The Nationwide Survey:
Research Design and Related Issues

The major study in the series reported here was a nationwide, epidemiologically oriented survey of one specific segment of physically abused children — the segment of children whose physical abuse was reported through legal channels of the states and U.S. territories during 1967 and 1968. It should be noted that extrapolations of findings from this survey beyond this clearly circumscribed segment may not be appropriate.

For purposes of the survey physical abuse of children was defined broadly on the basis of the behavior of perpetrators in accordance with the conceptual definition suggested in Chapter I, rather than narrowly, on the basis of injuries sustained by children, as was done for purposes of the public-opinion survey discussed in Chapter III. It will be recalled that the essential element in the conceptual definition is the intention of the perpetrator. For this reason the survey included incidents involving intentional acts of both commission and omission (for example, malnutrition resulting from intentional withholding of food). Incidents of sexual abuse, unless they also involved elements of nonsexual physical abuse, were excluded from this survey.

The survey was initiated in 1965, at a time when all the states of the United States were moving swiftly toward the enactment of legislation that required or encouraged physicians and others to report incidents of suspected child abuse to appropriate public authorities. As mentioned earlier, the enactment of such legislation had been suggested by the Children's Bureau in 1963 as a measure supposedly conducive to the protection of children from further abuse, and was promoted by the Bureau and other organizations so effectively that by the end of 1966 every state, with the exception of Hawaii, had passed its own version of a child-abuse reporting law, and Congress had enacted such a law for Washington, D.C. Hawaii passed its law early in 1967.

The new reporting laws seemed to accord with the concepts of the survey and were therefore seized upon as a central mechanism for its implementation. This survey was intended to collect data on a relatively large cohort of abused children, selected on a much broader basis than had been possible in earlier studies, which had usually obtained samples from one hospital or one agency. The main reason for obtaining a relatively large and broadly based study cohort was the assumption that the phenomenon of child abuse was likely to consist of different types, and that the chance for as many of these types as possible, and especially for low frequency types, to be included in a study cohort would increase as the cohort increased in size and as the framework for its selection was broadened. These desirable conditions seemed inherent in the utilization of legal reporting channels for the recruitment of a study cohort.

There are, however, certain shortcomings in linking a survey of abused children to legal reporting mechanisms of the states. Because of this linkage the survey was not expected to include all incidents of physical abuse of children but only those which for some reason entered the legal reporting channels. Since nothing definite is as yet known concerning the ratio of reported to unreported incidents, nor concerning factors associated with reporting and failure to report, it is impossible to draw reliable quantitative and qualitative inferences from reported to unreported cases. To obtain information on the unreported segment of the child-abuse spectrum, it would be necessary to employ different research approaches, such as a survey of randomly selected households.

A further shortcoming of the procedure employed in this survey is the fact that the reporting laws of the states and territories are not uniform, but differ on such important issues as the definition of the term "child," the definition of reportable circumstances, the designation of individuals and organizations responsible for reporting and for receiving reports, and the requirements for action to be taken once a report is made. In addition to differences in the codified provisions of the laws, there are marked differences in compliance rates with the law between states and within states. Furthermore, as with phenomena reportable in accordance with a law such as one dealing with venereal diseases and delinquency, certain systematic biases may affect compliance with reporting requirements at any level of the reporting system. Finally, the reporting laws of all the states in force at the time of the survey, with the exception of Arkansas, Hawaii, and Oregon, did not include medical examiners or coroners among those required to report suspected physical child abuse, nor did the laws require specifically reporting of fatalities. As a result of this legislative oversight, fatalities due to physical abuse of children were likely to be underrepresented among the legally reported cases of child abuse.

Study Procedures

The nationwide survey was originally scheduled to be conducted for one whole year starting on January 1, 1967. All the states,

Washington, D.C., Puerto Rico, and the Virgin Islands participated in the survey by submitting standardized information on
every incident of child abuse reported under their respective legislation. The Commonwealth of Puerto Rico participated, although it had no reporting legislation. Halfway through the
study year all participating jurisdictions were invited to extend
the survey through a second year. The response to this invitation
was unanimously positive, and it was therefore decided to continue reporting to the end of 1968, in order to obtain comparable
data for two successive years.

The 1967 survey was carried out on two levels: a basic level
involving every case reported in every locality throughout the
U.S. (with the exception of Philadelphia), and a more comprehensive level involving every case reported in a representative
sample of cities and counties.

The 1968 survey was carried out only on the basic level,
which by then did include Philadelphia.

Central Registries of Child Abuse

The basic mechanism for data collection on both levels of the
survey were central registries of child abuse which were established prior to its initiation in every state with the exception of
Texas. In several states, registries were set up in accordance
with state law. In all other states central registries were set up
especially for the survey, and procedures were developed for
channeling legal reports from every locality to the central registries and through them to the study office. Most state registries
agreed to use a standard, precoded Child Abuse Report form
which had been developed for the survey in order to report cases
to the study office. Some states utilized this form also for reporting from the local level to the state central registry as well as for
additional administrative purposes. A few states developed their
own Child Abuse Report forms, which were designed to corre-

spond to the standardized study form. Texas did not set up a separate mechanism for reporting incidents to the state level and to the study, since state authorities questioned the legality of these procedures. Instead, copies of the Texas standard child welfare forms on which a child-abuse code had been checked were forwarded by the Texas State Department of Welfare to the study office, and relevant information was then extracted from these forms. In California the study used, during 1967, copies of Police Crime Reports, which were forwarded by the legally established central registry in the Bureau of Criminal Identification and Investigation. Relevant information was extracted by the research staff from these crime reports and transferred to standard study forms. In 1968, at the suggestion of the staff of the study, the State Department of Social Welfare in California set up its own central registry in cooperation with the Bureau of Criminal Identification and Investigation and began using standard study forms for reporting incidents to the study office.

As can be seen, study procedures were set up in a flexible manner in response to legal and administrative patterns and program requirements of individual states, on the assumption that standardization of required information could be assured without insistence on uniformity of all formal procedures. In setting up procedures for the survey throughout the country, it seemed most important to strengthen the motivation and to assure the good will of all persons and offices participating in it. Such good will and motivation could be enhanced, it seemed, by gearing procedures flexibly to different local state requirements and capabilities.

The Report Form

The information collected by means of the standard child-abuse report form corresponded essentially to the information required under legislation of the states governing the reporting of child abuse. The abused child is identified by name and address and is described by age, sex, race, religion, and his relationship to the persons in whose custody he is living. The suspected perpetrator is identified and described by age, sex, race, religion, and his relationship to the abused child. The abusive incident is described by date, type of injury sustained, and circumstances leading up to and surrounding it. Information is provided also on the initial source reporting the incident and, if known, on previous abusive incidents involving the same child, the same family, or the same perpetrator. In addition, the report form included several items of administrative utility for local and state authorities. It should be noted that in order to avoid duplication of effort the form was designed to serve simultaneously the needs of research, service, administration, and law enforcement.

Except for one item, all items on the form were precoded to facilitate automated data processing. The forms used in 1967 and 1968 were identical as far as content is concerned, but, certain technical improvements were introduced in the 1968 form to simplify data processing: the 1967 form required two data cards, whereas the 1968 form could be punched onto one card without any loss of information. The forms are reproduced in Appendix A.

Case Screening and Editing

Every incident reported during the two study years in a local community under a given state's child-abuse reporting law was channeled to the study office via the state central registries. Since state reporting laws differ concerning the definition of the reportable phenomenon, the study received reports on cases which fit its conceptual definition of physical child abuse, as well as on cases which did not fit this definition. The primary task in editing reports prior to data processing was, therefore, to screen out cases which did not fit the conceptual definition. To assure reliability of this screening task, each report was read independently by two readers. In case of disagreement between these readers concerning a screening decision, the case was read by a third reader. In addition to the screening task editing the reports involved also checking for accuracy, completeness, and internal consistency. This, too, was done by two reader-editors, to ensure reliability. Occasionally reports had to be returned to the states to obtain missing information or to clear up inconsistencies. Editing also involved the extracting of relevant data from report forms of states which did not use the standard report forms of the study, and transcribing these data to the standard forms. California (only in 1967), Nevada, North Carolina, Pennsylvania, Texas, and Wisconsin (only in 1968) are the states that did not use the standard study forms.

Follow-Up Procedures

Incidents reported from the local level to a state central registry and from a state central registry to the study office could be cases of *suspected* rather than *established* child abuse. While in some instances it may not ever be possible to find out the true circumstances, investigation subsequent to initial reporting may frequently provide more definite information. It seemed important to eliminate from central registries in the states and from the study cohort cases which, upon investigation, turn out not to have involved physical abuse of children. Since it was not possible in many instances to differentiate between suspected and established abuse on the basis of material included in the original reports, a follow-up mechanism was designed, and states were asked to use it as a check for their own registries as well as for the nationwide registry at the study office. This mechanism involved classifying each case after investigation on the local level on a follow-up card, which was issued by the study office on every case submitted to it as one of suspected abuse. The classification on the follow-up card was:

1. Abuse confirmed
2. Abuse ruled out
3. Uncertain

If abuse was ruled out, reasons for the decision were indicated on the card for further classification by staff of the study. As can be seen, this mechanism provided no final resolution, since a number of the cases remained "uncertain." However, the mechanism assured the elimination of at least clear-cut nonabuse cases, which seemed important not only for purposes of research but also for the protection of the civil rights of individuals who were suspected and registered with state central registries even though they had not abused a child.

All the states with the exception of California, Texas, and Wisconsin participated in the follow-up procedures. During 1968 follow-up procedures were incorporated into the child-abuse report form to avoid separate follow-up procedures for cases concerning which the necessary information was already available at the point of initial reporting.

Comprehensive Study

In order to obtain more comprehensive data than were collected by means of the standard child-abuse report forms on every incident, all cases reported from forty cities and counties were to be subjected to a more thorough analysis. These cities and counties were selected from the official 1966 listing of Standard Metropolitan Statistical Areas. Core cities of the ten largest SMSA's were included in the sample by arbitrary decision, and thirty core cities and noncore counties were included on the basis of random selection from strata defined by population size and geographic region. The sample design and stratification criteria are reproduced in Appendix B. Of the ten largest cities two, Philadelphia and Washington, D.C., withdrew from the sample. Philadelphia was not able to participate in the 1967 study at all, and Washington, D.C., was not able to participate in the comprehensive level of the study. Eight areas that had been included in the sample reported no child-abuse cases during 1967. The area sample for comprehensive study was thus reduced to thirty units.

The sample units were limited intentionally to communities within Standard Metropolitan Statistical Areas not because of methodological and statistical considerations but because resources available to the study did not permit covering a more dispersed area sample. Since over 78 percent of all reported child-abuse incidents during 1967 occurred within SMSA's, however, the incidents subjected to comprehensive analysis are representative of nearly four fifths of the entire universe of reported 1967 incidents.

Inclusion of cases in the comprehensive study was controlled by the study office by means of Sample Unit Control and Follow-Up cards, which were prepared for each child whose home address on the standard report form identified him as living in a sample unit area. One copy of the card was sent to the administrator of the sampling unit to indicate that research schedules were to be completed for the child and perpetrator identified by the card, or that the card was to be returned to the study office if physical abuse was ruled out on the basis of local investigation. A second copy of the card was sent to the regional directors of the study to keep them informed on the composition of the comprehensive study sample in their respective regions. A third copy was kept at the study office as a control mechanism for data collection on sample cases.

Data collection in the sample communities was the responsibility of local, public, social welfare, child welfare, and probation departments whose staff members were directly involved in providing service for an abused child and his family. Research schedules for each abused child and his family and for each perpetrator or suspected perpetrator were completed by these staff members at the time the case was closed or by June 30, 1968 (six months after the termination of the study year) for cases still active at that time. The staff members involved in data collection were made familiar with the research schedules prior to the study year, so that they were aware in advance of their work with the sample cases of all the items on the schedules which were to be completed. Regional directors of the study visited sample communities at regular intervals to provide guidance to administrators, supervisors, and staff members of the local agencies; to assure compliance with study procedures; and, to the extent feasible, to assure the completeness and reliability of data collection. Assuring completeness and reliability of data involved, at times, returning schedules to sampling units whenever checking and editing by regional directors and by the study office revealed shortcomings or inconsistencies. In many communities the regional directors worked directly with caseworkers on schedule completion; in other communities they worked with supervisory and administrative personnel. Working arrangements in sample communities were developed flexibly to suit local administrative patterns. As can be expected, the quality of cooperation and performance of tasks varied from one sample community to another, yet, with a few exceptions, both were satisfactory.

It may be of interest to note that in several states social workers and probation officers who completed research schedules for the comprehensive segment of the survey were paid a per-unit fee for work they were asked to perform for the study. Arrangements for such fee payments were set up, in agreement with appropriate local and state authorities, whenever research schedules had to be completed as an additional task and on the staff members' own time, rather than on agency time as an integral aspect of the agency job. Offering recognition in the form of monetary rewards to individuals who performed a service for the study was expected to strengthen their motivation and to increase the reliability of their work. Apart from such considerations, however, it seemed only right to compensate individuals for extra work. Motivation of individuals participating in research, and reliability of task performance, are likely to depend on many factors. Monetary rewards may constitute only one of these factors, and their relative importance may be uncertain. Nevertheless, it seems that research designers may have to give more attention to monetary rewards for individuals who are expected to collect research data on their own time than has been given in the past.

Research Schedules

The three research schedules used for data collection for the comprehensive study are reproduced in Appendixes C, D, and E respectively.

As far as possible items included in the schedules explored factual rather than judgmental data. The main schedule described the abused child, his family, the abusive incident, medical treatment, social services, and official actions subsequent to the incident. The secondary schedule described the perpetrator. To prevent duplication of work on the part of the field staff, secondary schedules had to be completed only when the perpetrator was someone other than the child's parents or parent substitutes. If the child was abused by his parents or substitutes, transcription of information from the main to the perpetrator schedule was handled by the editing staff at the study office.

The third schedule was a special checklist of a set of circumstances that may or may not have been present in any given incident of physical child abuse. This list had been developed empirically on the basis of a content analysis of 140 child-abuse incidents from a pilot study conducted in California during 1966. The purpose of this checklist of circumstances was to provide data on a large sample of abused children as a basis for the development of an empirical typology of physical child abuse. The reliability and consistency of entries on this special schedule were checked during editing against an unstructured, open-ended description of circumstances leading up to and surrounding the abusive incident (item 26 of the main schedule).

The description of the abused child in the main schedule included, in addition to standard demographic items, questions on the child's school placement and on deviations in his physical, intellectual, and social functioning, as well as selected items on his past history, including previous involvement in abusive incidents. The description of the family included items on family and household structure; standard demographic items on parents or parent substitutes; questions on their educational, occupational, and socioeconomic status; questions on deviations in their physical, intellectual, and social functioning; selected items on their personal history, including past involvement in incidents of physical child abuse; and questions on housing and mobility. Several items explored also involvement in physical abuse of other children in the household. The abusive incident was described by items on timing and locality; the person or persons suspected as perpetrators, and their relationship to the child; others present during the incident; the injuries sustained by the child; the manner in which they were inflicted; and their degree of severity. Still other questions concerned steps taken after the incident by those involved in it and by health, welfare, and law enforcement authorities. Finally, individuals who completed the research schedules were asked to describe in detail, in their own words, the circumstances leading up to and surrounding the current incident. This item was the only nonstructured item of the schedules and was intended as a checking device for many structured items throughout the schedules, and especially for the separate schedule dealing with the circumstances of abuse.

The perpetrator schedule described the perpetrator in the

same way and through the same items in which the main schedule described the abused child's parents or substitutes and household.

Fatalities

During the early stages of this survey it was noted that incidents of physical abuse of children which resulted in a child's death were frequently not reported under child-abuse reporting mechanisms of the states. This underreporting of fatalities was in part due to inadequate wording or to too narrow and literal interpretation of reporting legislation. To obtain an estimate of the extent of this underreporting, a nationwide press survey of fatalities resulting from child abuse was conducted for six months from July through December 1967, simultaneously with the systematic survey of child-abuse incidents reported through legal channels.

Press coverage itself is not reliable in reporting the real scope of fatalities due to child abuse, since not all such incidents become known to the press, and of those that become known, not all may be considered newsworthy. Moreover, a press-clipping service may overlook some incidents reported in the press. In spite of these limitations, local press coverage seemed likely to approach comprehensiveness, and the clipping service, too, was expected to be more reliable concerning fatalities than concerning less severe incidents of child abuse.

As still another check on underreporting of fatalities due to child abuse, homicide statistics involving children were examined. These statistics are published regularly by the Mortality Statistics Branch, Division of Vital Statistics of the National Center for Health Statistics. However, since the Cause of Death tables do not specify the relationship between perpetrators and victims with respect to homicide incidents, the total figure for homicides of children includes incidents committed by caretakers as well as those by noncaretakers. A further limitation of the

Cause of Death tables is that some deaths of children which are classified as caused by accidents may not have been pure accidents but may have been caused by acts involving intentional abuse.

Pilot Study

In preparation for the nationwide survey a pilot study was conducted in California during 1966. The purpose of this pilot study was to test and adjust instruments and procedures which were to be used eventually in the nationwide survey, and to examine the feasibility of implementing the comprehensive level of that survey.

The pilot study was conducted in cooperation with the California State Department of Social Welfare and the newly established, official, statewide registry of child abuse in the Bureau of Criminal Investigation and Identification of the California State Department of Justice. A random sample was drawn consisting of 25 percent of all cases reported to the Bureau's registry from all police and sheriff's departments throughout the state during the first five months of operation of the registry. Detailed police reports on all cases in the sample were screened against the conceptual definition of physical abuse of children. Cases which fit the definition were then traced back to the communities in which they had occurred, and information concerning them was collected from public social and child welfare departments, courts, and hospitals who had known the children and adults involved, to the extent of offering them service and treatment. Data for the pilot study were collected by a member of the study staff rather than by staff members of local agencies. This was done in order to strengthen the reliability of the methodological component of the pilot study.

The universe explored by the pilot study consisted of 1676 officially reported incidents. The random sample included 421 incidents. Screening resulted in the elimination of 247 sample cases, which were classified as nonabuse, since they did not fit the conceptual definition developed by the study. Thirty-eight incidents had to be excluded from consideration, since they had been reported before the date on which the registry was established legally. Thirteen incidents had to be judged marginal, since data were insufficient to permit a clear decision concerning their status. The final sample of abuse cases of the pilot study consisted, therefore, of 123 incidents involving 140 children.

Substantive findings of the pilot study were published in 1968.[1] It is noteworthy that these findings foreshadowed in many ways eventual findings of the nationwide survey.

As mentioned earlier, data on circumstances of child abuse obtained through the California pilot study were subsequently used in the construction of the third schedule of the nationwide survey, the schedule which was to serve as a source in the development of an empirical typology of physical child abuse.

Analysis of Findings

Analysis of data collected in the nationwide survey focused on discerning associations between the phenomenon of physical child abuse and selected characteristics of abused children, their families, perpetrators of abuse, and the circumstances surrounding abuse. A secondary focus of analysis was in official acts of health, welfare, and law enforcement authorities subsequent to the reporting of child-abuse incidents. Finally, the analysis attempted to derive from the data a typology of circumstances of child abuse.

Data analysis was carried out at the Harvard University Computing Center on an IBM 7094 computer by means of the Data

1. David G. Gil, "California Pilot Study," in Helfer and Kempe, pp. 216–225.

Text program. This program is a computation system developed especially for the analysis of social science data by Arthur S. Couch of the Department of Social Relations at Harvard.[2] The principal statistical methods employed were cross-tabulations and tests of association concerning variables, the relationships and interaction effects of which appeared relevant to the analysis. In developing the typology of circumstances of child abuse, a factor analysis was carried out of data collected by means of the special schedule on circumstances.[3]

Study Resources

Important factors underlying the quality of any study are the resources at the disposal of the researcher. Discussions of the design of studies should, therefore, provide information on these

2. Couch, *Data-Text System — A Computer Language for Social Science Research,* mimeographed (Department of Social Relations, Harvard University, 1967).

3. The factor analysis and rotations were carried out by the Data-Text System. The factor analysis program of this system calculates Hotelling's Principal Component Solution, according to the procedures outlined in H. H. Harman, *Modern Factor Analysis* (Chicago, Universtiy of Chicago Press, 1960), pp. 154–191. The Standard Power Method is used in the iterative computations, which are carried out to an accuracy of six decimal places, or to the accuracy achieved from a maximum of 200 iterations. For the purpose of improving the speed of convergence, the iterative process is aided by Aitken's Delta Square Method of acceleration. See V. N. Faddeeva, *Computational Methods of Linear Algebra* (New York, Dover Press, 1959), pp. 202–219. The Rotational Program of the Data-Text System consists of a variety of orthogonal rotations on factor loadings and factor scores. Both Analytic type rotations and Fixed Position type rotations are available. The Analytic rotations of the Data-Text System were designed to be a mathematical approximation of the simple-structure criteria proposed in L. L. Thurstone, *Multiple Factor Analysis* (Chicago, University of Chicago Press, 1947). The procedure for these analytic rotations are described in Harman, *Modern Factor Analysis,* chapter 14. Of the various analytic type rotations available in the Data-Text program, the Normal Orthogonal Varimax Rotation was selected for the present study. This method attempts to simplify the columns of the factor matrix. During the rotational procedure factor loadings are transformed so that each variable has unit communality — that is, each variable is weighted equally regardless of its actual communality.

resources so that other researchers may judge design aspects in relation to this reality factor, and also in order to make this information available to researchers contemplating the utilization of similar designs.

The total cost of the series of studies reported in this book during the four-year period, July 1965 through June 1969, was approximately $500,000, 80 percent of which was for direct costs.[4] A major portion of the direct costs, $275,000, was spent on salaries for professional, technical, and clerical staff. Transportation and communications, another major item in view of the nationwide scope of the study, amounted to approximately $50,000. The rest of the direct costs, approximately $75,000, was for fees for completion of research schedules in sample areas, data-processing and computations, the NORC public-opinion survey, press-clipping service, and consumable supplies.

Professional staff during the first six months consisted of one person, the study director, who developed during that stage overall plans for the studies and also negotiated the entree into the participating states and agencies. During the second half of the first year two more professionals joined the study staff, one to implement the pilot study in California and the other to assist in overall planning, administration, and design. These two professionals left the staff during the second year, when their respective assignments terminated.

At the beginning of the second year three field directors joined the staff, each of whom assumed responsibility for the implementation of the basic survey in seventeen states and the implemen-

4. The term "direct costs" refers to that part of the authorized research budget which is actually available for the purchase of study resources, such as staff, transportation, communications, equipment, consumable supplies, data processing, etc. "Indirect costs" are not available for study resources but are for overhead costs of the institution that houses the study. The rate of indirect cost is determined by agencies of the federal government which sponsor and support a given study on the basis of annual institutional audits. For the present series of studies the rate of indirect cost was set at 20 percent of direct costs.

tation of the comprehensive level of the survey in thirteen sample areas located in these states. All three regional directors stayed with the study for three years until the termination of field operations. These three professionals constituted the basic quality control mechanism in the implementation of the study, since compliance with predetermined study procedures on the part of staff members of participating states and local agencies was assured by means of the facilitating and supervisory actions taken by the field directors. It is possible that the reliability of the survey could have been increased had the quantitative responsibility of the field directors been reduced by increasing their number. This illustrates the aforementioned relationship between the quality of a study and the resources at its disposal.

In selection of field directors, attempts were made to recruit mature and experienced professionals capable of working with a high degree of independence and initiative. They were encouraged by the study director to develop their individual style in carrying out their defined responsibilities. Administrative regulations were kept at a minimum, since what mattered was the product of their work and not the manner in which each of them went about producing it. This liberal approach to field-staff supervision gave the study director occasional nightmares, but it paid off in the long run. The field directors enjoyed the freedom of their working conditions, they were highly motivated and enthusiastic about their role, and they delivered the product.

It should be noted that salaries for the field directors were set by design above the salary range for individuals with comparable education and experience. By setting such high salary levels it was possible to attract a large number of candidates for the three positions and to select those whose qualifications ensured the reliability of the data collected. This salary policy resulted in an additional cost of approximately $18,000 over three years. In retrospect this seems to have been a wise investment, for it may have prevented the loss of the total $500,000 investment in this study.

The technical staff of the study consisted of a secretary and several research assistants whoe role was to screen, check, and edit the various research schedules as they arrived at the study office from the field and to prepare follow-up and control cards for the field units. Each schedule was screened, checked, and edited by at least two readers, each working independently. Two research assistants were also trained keypunch operators and were responsible for punching data from the edited research schedules onto IBM cards. The study had at its disposal an IBM keypunch, an IBM verifier, and an IBM counter-sorter. To assure accuracy and reliability of data punching, each data card was verified by a second keypunch operator. The number of research assistants varied over the years of the study from one to five, depending on changes in flow of data from the field.

The study enjoyed a high degree of staff stability. There was no turnover at all among the professional staff and minimal turnover among research assistants.

Dissemination and Utilization of Findings

One final issue to be examined in a chapter dealing with questions of design and method concerns the provisions made in the course of the study for the dissemination and utilization of eventual findings. Government agencies and philanthropic foundations who sponsor social science research are, rightfully, quite concerned with this issue. Dissemination and utilization of research findings is likely to depend on many factors, some of which only may be subject to influence by research designers. It seems that research designers can facilitate eventual utilization of their findings if they foster open and honest communication throughout the planning stage and execution of their studies with various segments of the public who may be expected later on to make use of the findings. Such a policy of openness results in certain costs in terms of staff work and time, but these costs should be viewed as worthwhile investments if dissemination and utilization of research findings is indeed taken seriously.

A policy of open communication was adopted from the outset of this series of studies. The study and its emerging findings were discussed at numerous national and statewide meetings of professional organizations concerned with child abuse. In addition to presenting papers at conferences and arranging for their subsequent publication in appropriate professional journals, the study director responded liberally to mail requests for papers and information from several hundred individuals and agencies from the United States and abroad as well as from the press, radio, and television.

Another potentially constructive approach to dissemination and utilization of research findings is the direct involvement in the study of professional practitioners and of agencies to whose work the findings are likely to be relevant. Such involvement and participation were built into the design of the child-abuse surveys. Not only were the data for the survey collected by professional practitioners who carried service responsibilities for abused children and their families, but the instruments used in data collection were designed in a manner that was intended to be meaningful for practice as well as research. Staff members of agencies in several sample areas were therefore introduced by the study staff to new and systematic approaches to analyzing child-abuse cases. The study consequently had a direct and immediate impact on practice, especially in the sample areas.

The study, in addition to its direct impact on practitioners, affected administrative patterns of state agencies. Central registries of child abuse were developed in all states even though legal requirements to establish such registries existed in a few states only. Many states decided to maintain and utilize these registries beyond the termination of the survey. State authorities and local agencies received regular reports from the study office on child abuse throughout the country, which enabled them to view the situation in their own state in relation to other states. The field directors of the study acted to a certain extent as an unofficial channel of communication between state agencies concerning practice developments with respect to incidents of child abuse. These various by-products of the study process enabled many state and local agencies to examine their policies and procedures concerning child abuse in a more systematic manner than would have been the case had they not been involved with the implementation of the survey.

Chapter Five

The Nationwide Survey Findings

Central registries in the states and U.S. territories forwarded 9,563 child-abuse reports to the survey during 1967 and 10,931 reports during 1968. Screening these reports against the conceptual definition of physical abuse of children resulted in the elimination of 3,570 reports, or 37.33 percent from the 1967 sample, and 4,314 reports, or 39.47 percent from the 1968 sample. Consequently, the study samples of physically abused children were reduced to 5,993 children for 1967 and 6,617 children for 1968.

Table 12 classifies all reports received by the survey for 1967 and 1968 into abuse and nonabuse cases for each state and territory. Table 13 shows the size of the total resident population, the number of children under age 18 in this population, and the rate of reported incidents of physical child abuse per 100,000 children under age 18 for each state.

Table 12. Classification of Reports Received from Central Registries during 1967 and 1968

	1967			1968		
State	All Reports	Abuse	Non-abuse	All Reports	Abuse	Non-abuse
United States	9,563	5,993	3,570	10,931	6,617	4,314
Alabama	44	38	6	43	34	9
Alaska	10	8	2	11	10	1
Arizona	18	16	2	2	2	0
Arkansas	16	13	3	20	17	3
California	3,683	1,357	2,326	4,016	1,258	2,758
Colorado	100	81	19	78	67	11
Connecticut	87	77	10	78	73	5
Delaware	27	26	1	16	13	3
Wash., D.C.	30	27	3	37	26	11
Florida	29	26	3	10	9	1
Georgia	70	50	20	62	55	7
Hawaii	71	60	11	42	35	7
Idaho	17	12	5	2	2	0
Illinois	435	313	122	494	376	118
Indiana	106	94	12	125	124	1
Iowa	112	80	32	186	132	54
Kansas	26	22	4	61	58	3
Kentucky	93	83	10	40	34	6
Louisiana	29	24	5	14	13	1
Maine	9	9	0	5	4	1
Maryland	401	271	130	504	324	180
Massachusetts	124	113	11	156	114	42
Michigan	476	334	142	721	539	182
Minnesota	70	60	10	107	95	12
Mississippi	22	17	5	23	22	1
Missouri	104	87	17	72	54	18
Montana	23	20	3	11	8	3
Nebraska	7	7	0	16	16	0
Nevada	25	20	5	39	31	8
New Hampshire	25	25	0	23	20	3
New Jersey	80	59	21	50	37	13
New Mexico	22	21	1	13	13	0
New York	701	431	270	989	574	415
North Carolina	136	89	47	155	102	53
North Dakota	2	2	0	2	2	0

Table 12 (*continued*)

State	1967 All Reports	Abuse	Non-abuse	1968 All Reports	Abuse	Non-abuse
Ohio	197	166	31	146	128	18
Oklahoma	41	38	3	12	12	0
Oregon	59	58	1	30	30	0
Pennsylvania	343[a]	259[a]	84[a]	555	385	170
Rhode Island	0	0	0	0	0	0
South Carolina	32	24	8	41	38	3
South Dakota	6	4	2	0	0	0
Tennessee	111	75	36	116	72	44
Texas	998	987	11	1,282	1,282	0
Utah	31	21	10	27	17	10
Vermont	5	4	1	7	6	1
Virginia	82	12	70	48	35	13
Washington	110	110	0	122	81	41
West Virginia	52	41	11	16	15	1
Wisconsin	220	186	34	296	213	83
Wyoming	18	14	4	4	4	0
Puerto Rico[b]	26	20	6	1	1	0
Virgin Islands	2	2	0	5	5	0

[a] Not including Philadelphia.
[b] Puerto Rico had no child-abuse reporting legislation.

Table 13. Rates of Reported Incidents of Physical Abuse per 100,000
Children under Age 18

State	Total Resident Population in Thous.[a]	1967 Children under Age 18 in Thous.[a]	Rate per 100,000 Children under Age 18	Total Resident Population in Thous.[b]	1968 Children under Age 18 in Thous.[b]	Rate per 100,000 Children under Age 18
United States (excluding Puerto Rico & Virgin Is.)	197,861	70,775	8.4	199,861	70,809	9.3
Alabama	3,540	1,323	2.8	3,558	1,309	2.5
Alaska	272	118	6.7	274	120	8.3
Arizona	1,634	646	2.4	1,663	650	0.3
Arkansas	1,968	710	1.8	1,986	706	2.4
California	19,153	6,769	20.0	19,300	6,764	18.5
Colorado	1,975	727	11.1	2,043	741	9.0
Connecticut	2,925	1,009	7.6	2,963	1,017	7.1
Delaware	523	198	13.1	534	198	6.5
Wash., D.C.	809	281	9.6	809	282	9.2
Florida	5,995	2,051	1.2	6,151	2,094	0.4
Georgia	4,509	1,702	2.9	4,568	1,706	3.2
Hawaii	739	288	20.8	780	301	11.6
Idaho	699	266	4.5	703	264	0.7
Illinois	10,893	3,836	8.1	10,991	3,860	9.7
Indiana	5,000	1,833	5.1	5,061	1,840	6.7
Iowa	2,753	978	8.1	2,774	972	13.5
Kansas	2,275	803	2.7	2,293	795	7.2
Kentucky	3,189	1,152	7.2	3,220	1,140	2.9
Louisiana	3,662	1,460	1.6	3,726	1,465	0.8
Maine	973	350	2.5	976	347	1.1
Maryland	3,682	1,356	19.9	3,754	1,375	23.5
Massachusetts	5,421	1,853	6.0	5,469	1,850	6.1
Michigan	8,584	3,230	10.3	8,739	3,260	16.5
Minnesota	3,582	1,349	4.4	3,647	1,356	7.0
Mississippi	2,348	934	1.8	2,344	921	2.3
Missouri	4,603	1,574	5.5	4,625	1,567	3.4
Montana	701	266	7.5	693	261	3.0
Nebraska	1,435	517	1.3	1,439	512	3.1
Nevada	444	169	11.8	449	172	18.0
New Hampshire	686	241	10.3	702	244	8.1
New Jersey	7,003	2,369	2.4	7,093	2,380	1.5
New Mexico	1,003	435	4.8	1,006	431	3.0
New York	18,336	6,037	7.1	18,078	5,944	9.6
North Carolina	5,029	1,842	4.8	5,122	1,845	5.5
North Dakota	639	245	0.8	627	236	0.8
Ohio	10,458	3,798	4.3	10,588	3,805	3.3
Oklahoma	2,495	842	4.5	2,520	842	1.4
Oregon	1,999	684	8.4	2,008	678	4.4
Pennsylvania	11,629	3,893	6.6[c]	11,728	3,880	9.9
Rhode Island	900	300	0.0	914	298	0.0
South Carolina	2,599	1,012	2.3	2,664	1,018	3.7
South Dakota	674	257	1.5	656	247	0.0
Tennessee	3,892	1,374	5.4	3,975	1,383	5.2
Texas	10,869	4,101	24.0	10,977	4,099	31.2
Utah	1,024	431	4.8	1,034	432	3.9
Vermont	417	151	2.6	425	150	4.0
Virginia	4,536	1,635	0.7	4,595	1,643	2.1
Washington	3,087	1,086	10.1	3,276	1,138	7.1
West Virginia	1,798	621	6.6	1,802	607	2.4
Wisconsin	4,189	1,553	11.9	4,221	1,546	13.7
Wyoming	315	119	11.7	315	118	3.3

[a] U.S. Bureau of the Census, Current Population Reports, Series P-25, No. 384.

[b] Ibid., No. 420.

[c] Excluding Philadelphia.

Levels and Rates of Reporting

Tables 12 and 13 reveal a net increase of 10.41 percent in the annual count of reported incidents of physical child abuse from 1967 to 1968. The tables reveal also changes, up and downward, in reporting rates per 100,000 children under age 18 for individual states from one year to the next, and differences in reporting rates between the states for each of the two years of the survey. In examining the meaning of the net increase, the intrastate changes, and the interstate differences, it is important to recall that the survey dealt only with the reported segment, and not with the real incidence, of child abuse.

The net increase in the annual count of reported child-abuse incidents should not be interpreted as reflecting an increase in their real incidence. Rather, this increase seems to reflect changes in administrative concern with child abuse and other administrative and legal factors. 1967 had been for many states the first full year of reporting and of administering central registries. Procedures were still being tested and modified, and reporting laws were still being amended and strengthened during that first year. Laws, regulations, and procedures had become more firmly established by the second year of the survey.

The net increase of 624 reports resulted from an increase of 1,157 reports in 22 states and the Virgin Islands, and a decrease of 533 reports in 26 states, Washington, D.C., and Puerto Rico. Reporting levels remained unchanged during the study years in two states. Table 14, which lists increases and decreases in reporting levels and rates for each state, shows that nearly half the net increase for the country originated in Texas. Reliability of reporting from this state was especially low, since Texas was the only state that failed to establish a central registry of child abuse for the survey,[1] did not participate in follow-up investigation of

1. Texas amended its reporting legislation in 1969 and in accordance with it established an official central registry in the Department of Public Welfare as of September 1, 1969.

Table 14. Changes in Levels and Rates of Reporting from 1967 to 1968[a]

| | Increases | | | Decreases | |
| | | Rate per 100,000 Children under | | | Rate per 100,000 Children under |
State	Number +	Age 18 +	State	Number −	Age 18 −
Alaska	2	0.9	Alabama	4	0.3
Arkansas	4	0.6	Arizona	14	2.1
Georgia	5	0.3	California	99	1.5
Illinois	63	1.6	Colorado	14	2.1
Indiana	30	1.6	Connecticut	4	0.5
Iowa	52	5.4	Delaware	13	6.6
Kansas	36	4.5	Wash., D.C.	1	0.4
Maryland	53	3.6	Florida	17	0.8
Massachusetts	1	0.1	Hawaii	25	9.2
Michigan	205	6.2	Idaho	10	3.8
Minnesota	35	2.6	Kentucky	49	4.3
Mississippi	5	0.5	Louisiana	11	0.8
Nebraska	9	1.8	Maine	5	1.4
Nevada	11	6.2	Missouri	33	2.1
New York	143	2.5	Montana	12	4.5
North Carolina	13	0.7	New Hampshire	5	2.2
Pennsylvania	126	3.3	New Jersey	22	0.9
South Carolina	14	1.4	New Mexico	8	1.8
Texas	295	7.2	Ohio	38	1.0
Vermont	2	1.4	Oklahoma	26	3.1
Virginia	23	1.4	Oregon	28	4.0
Wisconsin	27	1.8	South Dakota	4	1.5
Virgin Islands	3	not available	Tennessee	3	0.2
			Utah	4	0.9
			Washington	29	3.0
			West Virginia	26	4.2
			Wyoming	10	8.4
			Puerto Rico	19	not available
Total	1,157		Total	533	
United States	624	0.9			

[a] No changes were registered for North Dakota and Rhode Island.

cases on the local level, and did not provide to the survey sufficient, standardized information to permit screening of reports against the conceptual definition of physical child abuse.

Over one fifth of the net increase in reporting came from Pennsylvania. However, almost the entire increase in that state's reporting level resulted from the participation of Philadelphia in the 1968 survey. This city had not submitted reports to the study during 1967. In 1968, 109 incidents were reported from Philadelphia.

Marked increases in reporting levels occurred in Maryland and New York and in the following states of the Midwest: Illinois, Indiana, Iowa, Kansas, Michigan, Minnesota, Nebraska, and Wisconsin. Among Southern states North and South Carolina and Virginia registered moderate increases in reporting. Most of the states that registered these increases had taken administrative action to strengthen reporting procedures.

More than half the states registered minor, moderate, or marked decreases in reporting levels and rates. This group includes most of the states in the South and the West. Observations of survey field staff indicated that as a group, these states have shown less administrative concern and initiative with respect to child-abuse reporting than the states which registered increases in reporting levels. The decrease thus seems to have been a consequence of a different administrative approach.

Differences in reporting rates per 100,000 children between individual states during each year of the survey should not be interpreted without more specific evidence as a reflection of real interstate differences in the incidence of child abuse, although the existence of such real differences cannot be ruled out on the basis of data of the surveys. Analogous to the argument made earlier concerning intrastate changes in levels of reporting over time, the most appropriate interpretation of interstate differences in reporting rates seems to be that they are primarily a function of differences in reporting legislation, in professional and public concern with child abuse, and in the effectiveness of administrative procedures concerning the implementation of reporting legislation.

Reporting rates range from as high as 31.2 reports per 100,-000 children for Texas in 1968 to as low as no reports at all for Rhode Island during both years of the survey. The rate for the entire United States was 8.4 reports per 100,000 children for

1967 and 9.3 reports for 1968. Changes in population figures from 1967 to 1968 were taken into consideration in calculating the rates.

Table 15 ranks all states by reporting rates per 100,000 children for each of the study years, and Table 16 summarizes the data. Inspection of these tables reveals a high degree of stability of this rank order from one year to the next, although marked changes occurred in the ranks of some states and in the reporting rates from which the ranks were derived. The relative stability of the rank orders is confirmed also by statistical analysis. The coefficient of rank order correlation, Spearman's r_s, between the rank order of the states for 1967 and 1968 respectively is .809.[2] The meaning of stability of rank order is that reporting patterns of individual states over time were relatively stable in relation to other states, but not that they were stable in absolute terms. The extent of absolute change of reporting rates per 100,000 children for individual states from 1967 to 1968 was, however, also rather small, as can be seen from Table 17.

The examination of absolute reporting levels and relative rates suggests that reporting patterns of physical abuse of children do not parallel the distribution of the United States population, and that these patterns tend to be relatively stable over time. When shifts do occur in the patterns, they seem related to changes in legal, professional, and administrative factors. This observed relationship between changes in reporting patterns and legal, professional, and administrative factors indicates that these factors are an important determinant of reporting levels and rates. However, alternative interpretations of the observed reporting patterns are not ruled out on the basis of data available so far. There is a possibility that regional differences in real incidence of physical child abuse and in child-rearing practices may be

2. Hubert M. Blalock, *Social Statistics* (New York, Toronto, London, McGraw-Hill, 1960), pp. 317–319. In the present case the coefficient of rank correlation of .809 has a standard deviation of .141 and a standard score, $z = 5.738$. It is therefore significant at the .000001 level.

Table 15. Ranking of States by Reporting Rates per 100,000 Children under Age 18

Rank No.	State	Rate	Rank No.	State	Rate
	1967			*1968*	
1	Texas	24.0	1	Texas	31.2
2	Hawaii	20.8	2	Maryland	23.5
3	California	20.0	3	California	18.5
4	Maryland	19.9	4	Nevada	18.0
5	Delaware	13.1	5	Michigan	16.5
6	Wisconsin	11.9	6	Wisconsin	13.7
7	Nevada	11.8	7	Iowa	13.5
8	Wyoming	11.7	8	Hawaii	11.6
9	Colorado	11.1	9	Pennsylvania	9.9
10 }	Michigan	10.3	10	Illinois	9.7
11 }	New Hampshire	10.3	11	New York	9.6
12	Washington	10.1	12	Wash., D.C.	9.2
13	Wash., D.C.	9.6	13	Colorado	9.0
14	Oregon	8.4	14	Alaska	8.3
15 }	Illinois	8.1	15	New Hampshire	8.1
16 }	Iowa	8.1	16	Kansas	7.2
17	Connecticut	7.6	17 }	Connecticut	7.1
18	Montana	7.5	18 }	Washington	7.1
19	Kentucky	7.2	19	Minnesota	7.0
20	New York	7.1	20	Indiana	6.7
21	Alaska	6.7	21	Delaware	6.5
22 }	Pennsylvania	6.6	22	Massachusetts	6.1
23 }	West Virginia	6.6	23	North Carolina	5.5
24	Massachusetts	6.0	24	Tennessee	5.2
25	Missouri	5.5	25	Oregon	4.4
26	Tennessee	5.4	26	Vermont	4.0
27	Indiana	5.1	27	Utah	3.9
28 }	New Mexico	4.8	28	South Carolina	3.7
29 }	North Carolina	4.8	29	Missouri	3.4
30 }	Utah	4.8	30 }	Ohio	3.3
31 }	Idaho	4.5	31 }	Wyoming	3.3
32 }	Oklahoma	4.5	32	Georgia	3.2
33	Minnesota	4.4	33	Nebraska	3.1
34	Ohio	4.3	34 }	Montana	3.0
35	Georgia	2.9	35 }	New Mexico	3.0
36	Alabama	2.8	36	Kentucky	2.9
37	Kansas	2.7	37	Alabama	2.5
38	Vermont	2.6	38 }	Arkansas	2.4
39	Maine	2.5	39 }	West Virginia	2.4
40 }	Arizona	2.4	40	Mississippi	2.3
41 }	New Jersey	2.4	41	Virginia	2.1
42	South Carolina	2.3	42	New Jersey	1.5
43 }	Arkansas	1.8	43	Oklahoma	1.4
44 }	Mississippi	1.8	44	Maine	1.1
45	Louisiana	1.6	45 }	Louisiana	0.8
46	South Dakota	1.5	46 }	North Dakota	0.8
47	Nebraska	1.3	47	Idaho	0.7
48	Florida	1.2	48	Florida	0.4
49	North Dakota	0.8	49	Arizona	0.3
50	Virginia	0.7	50 }	Rhode Island	0.0
51	Rhode Island	0.0	51 }	South Dakota	0.0

Note: Rank No. 1 indicates highest rate. Coefficient of Rank Correlation between Rankings of 1967 and 1968 = .809.

Findings

Table 16. Ranking of States by Reporting Rates — Summary

State	Reporting Rate Rank 1967	Reporting Rate Rank 1968	State	Reporting Rate Rank 1967	Reporting Rate Rank 1968
Alabama	36	37	Montana	18	34.5
Alaska	21	14	Nebraska	47	33
Arizona	40.5	49	Nevada	7	4
Arkansas	43.5	38.5	New Hampshire	10.5	15
California	3	3	New Jersey	40.5	42
Colorado	9	13	New Mexico	29	34.5
Connecticut	17	17.5	New York	20	11
Delaware	5	21	North Carolina	29	23
Wash., D.C.	13	12	North Dakota	49	45.5
Florida	48	48	Ohio	34	30.5
Georgia	35	32	Oklahoma	31.5	43
Hawaii	2	8	Oregon	14	25
Idaho	31.5	47	Pennsylvania	22.5	9
Illinois	15.5	10	Rhode Island	51	50.5
Indiana	27	20	South Carolina	42	28
Iowa	15.5	7	South Dakota	46	50.5
Kansas	37	16	Tennessee	26	24
Kentucky	19	36	Texas	1	1
Louisiana	45	45.5	Utah	29	27
Maine	39	44	Vermont	38	26
Maryland	4	2	Virginia	50	41
Massachusetts	24	22	Washington	12	17.5
Michigan	10.5	5	West Virginia	22.5	38.5
Minnesota	33	19	Wisconsin	6	6
Mississippi	43.5	40	Wyoming	8	30.5
Missouri	25	29			

Note: Rank No. 1 indicates highest rate. Coefficient of Rank Correlation between Rankings for 1967 and 1968 = .809.

contributing factors to the observed deviation of reporting patterns from the population distribution.

One final comment with respect to reporting patterns concerns child-abuse reports from metropolitan and nonmetropolitan areas. The reporting rate in Standard Metropolitan Statistical

Table 17. Extent of Change in Reporting Rates per 100,000 Children
under Age 18

Extent of Change	Number of States	Number of States Cumulative
0.00	2	2
0.1 to 0.9	14	16
1.0 to 1.9	12	28
2.0 to 2.9	6	34
3.0 to 3.9	5	39
4.0 to 4.9	5	44
5.0 to 7.9	5	49
8.0 to 9.9	2	51

Areas (SMSA's) during both years of the survey was markedly
higher than in areas outside of SMSA's. Although about 67 percent of the United States population lived in SMSA's, 78.26
percent of the 1967 and 81.90 percent of the 1968 child-abuse
reports originated from communities within SMSA's. This concentration of reports in metropolitan areas and the stability of
that concentration support the view that administrative and professional factors exert an influence on reporting patterns. Administrative provisions and professional services for reporting and
dealing with physical abuse of children tend to be more concentrated in metropolitan areas than outside these areas.

Study Cohort and Sample Cohort

The terms "Study Cohort" and "Sample Cohort" will be used in
the following discussion of characteristics of abused children,
their families, and perpetrators to differentiate between data collected through the basic level of the 1967 and 1968 nationwide
surveys, and data collected through the comprehensive level of
the 1967 survey. The 1967 sample cohort consisted of 1,380
children, 23.03 percent of the 1967 study cohort, which numbered 5,993 children. The 1968 study cohort numbered 6,617
children. The 1968 survey was conducted only on the basic, na-

tionwide level, and there was thus no 1968 sample cohort. It is of interest to note, however, that 25.57 percent of the 1968 study cohort was reported from the cities and counties that constituted the sample communities of the 1967 survey. This is one further illustration of the stability of reporting patterns.

The distribution of the 1967 sample cohort among the sample communities is shown in Table 18.[3]

Table 18. Distribution of Sample Cohort by Sample Communities — 1967[a]

Sample Community	Number	Percent	Sample Community	Number	Percent
Los Angeles, Cal.	231	16.74	Du Page County, Ill.	2	0.14
San Francisco, Cal.	73	5.29	Columbus, Ohio	11	0.80
St. Louis City, Mo.	17	1.23	Dayton, Ohio	18	1.30
St. Louis County, Mo.	20	1.45	Summit County, Ohio	20	1.45
San Mateo County, Cal.	17	1.23	Madison, Wis.	4	0.29
Seattle, Wash.	26	1.88	Worcester County, Mass.	2	0.14
Oklahoma City, Okla.	12	0.87	New York City, N. Y.	282	20.43
Multnomah County, Ore.	2	0.14	Pittsburgh, Pa.	50	3.63
Lubbock, Texas	13	0.94	Westchester County, N. Y.	7	0.51
Boise City, Idaho	3	0.22	Prince Georges County, Md.	14	1.01
Maricopa County, Ariz.	3	0.22	Baltimore City, Md.	162	11.74
Chicago, Ill.	154	11.16	Louisville, Ky.	32	2.32
Detroit, Mich.	96	6.96	Baltimore County, Md.	9	0.65
Boston, Mass.	42	3.04	Nashville, Tenn.	24	1.74
Cook County, Ill.	28	2.03	Macon, Georgia	6	0.43
			Total	1,380	100.00

[a] No child-abuse incidents were reported during 1967 from the following eight communities, which had been selected as sample communities: Osage County, Oklahoma; Taylor County, Texas; Clermont County, Ohio; Fargo, North Dakota; Middlesex County, Connecticut; Wayne County, New York; Palm Beach County, Florida; Fayette County, Kentucky.

Nonabuse Cases. Before discussion of the physical abuse cases of the study and sample cohorts, some comments seem indicated on the nature of the nonphysical abuse cases that were reported to state registries but were excluded from the study. An analysis of the 3,570 "screened-out" reports from the 1967 survey revealed that nearly one half were cases of neglect. This was to be expected, since neglect is included in the definition of reportable

3. Eight of the originally selected sample communities did not report child-abuse incidents during 1967.

circumstances under child-abuse reporting legislation of many states. Over one sixth of the reports were incidents of sexual abuse, 10.3 percent were accidents, 4.3 percent were cases resulting from illness, 3.4 percent were incidents of physical abuse inflicted by persons not in a caretaker relationship to the victim, 13.3 percent were false reports, and 3.1 percent were classified as "other" circumstances. The distribution of 1968 nonabuse cases among the foregoing categories was similar to the one reported for 1967.

Characteristics of Abused Children, Their Families, and the Perpetrators

Sex and Age. Slightly more than half the children in both study cohorts were boys, 52.6 percent in 1967 and 51.2 percent in 1968. Analysis of the sex distribution of different age groups revealed, however, that although boys outnumbered girls in every age group below age 12, they were outnumbered by girls among the teen-aged victims of child abuse, 63.3 percent as against 36.7 percent in 1967 and 63.8 percent as against 36.2 percent in 1968.

Changes in sex distribution of victims of child abuse during different stages of childhood and adolescence seem to reflect culturally determined child-rearing attitudes. Girls tend to be viewed as more conforming than boys throughout childhood, and physical force tends to be used less frequently in rearing them. However, during stages of sexual maturation parental anxieties concerning their daughters' heterosexual relationships lead to increasing restrictions, intensified conflicts, and increasing use of physical force in asserting parental control. With respect to boys the pattern seems different. Physical force tends to be used more readily throughout childhood to assure conformity. During adolescence, however, as the physical strength of boys increases and often matches or even surpasses their parents' strength, the use of physical force in disciplining boys tends to diminish.

Table 19 shows the age distribution of the study cohorts.

Table 19. Age Distribution of Children

Age Group	1967 Study Cohort N = 5993		1968 Study Cohort N = 6617	
	Percent	*Cum. Percent*	*Percent*	*Cum. Percent*
Under 6 months	8.0	8.0	8.1	8.1
6 mos. to under 1 year	5.8	13.8	5.5	13.6
1 to under 2 years	10.0	23.8	10.8	24.4
2 to under 3 years	9.4	33.2	9.4	33.8
3 to under 6 years	20.1	53.3	19.9	53.7
6 to under 9 years	18.2	71.5	15.1	68.8
9 to under 12 years	11.4	82.9	12.2	81.0
12 to under 15 years	10.6	93.5	10.8	91.8
15 and over	6.3	99.8	5.6	97.4
Age unknown	—	—	2.6	100.0

The age distributions of both study cohorts suggest that physical abuse of children is not limited to very young children as has been suggested by numerous investigators. Over three quarters of the children in both cohorts were over two years of age, and nearly half the children were over six years. Nearly one fifth were teen-agers and, as just reported, the majority of the teen-agers were girls. The age distribution was similar for all ethnic groups.

The findings of many earlier studies, according to which most abused children are very young, seem to have resulted from bias in the selection and composition of study groups. Most of these studies were conducted in medical settings where, because of the function of the setting, more severely injured abused children are seen. In the comprehensive level of the 1967 survey it was found that younger children of the sample cohort tended to be more severely injured than older ones. Sixty-five percent of children under age three but only 35 percent over that age were severely or fatally injured. It is therefore to be expected that younger and more severely injured children will be overrepresented in study samples of abused children selected from hospital populations.

Ethnicity. About one third of the children of each study cohort were nonwhite. Since only 15 percent of children under age 18 in the United States were nonwhite in 1967, nonwhites were overrepresented in the study cohorts to a significant extent. In 1968 the reporting rate for white children was 6.7 per 100,000, and the corresponding rate for nonwhite children was 21.0. The proportion of nonwhite children was even higher, 60.8 percent, in the 1967 sample cohort, which was drawn from metropolitan areas and included nine of the country's largest cities, all of which have a higher concentration of nonwhites than the population as a whole. More specifically, of the 1,380 children of the sample cohort 38.8 percent were white, 45.7 percent Negro, 0.7 percent American Indian, 6.7 percent Puerto Rican, 4.1 percent Mexican, 0.7 percent Asian, 3.0 percent other, and in 0.4 percent the ethnic background was not reported.

The marked overrepresentation of nonwhite children in the study and sample cohorts may reflect several underlying factors and the interaction between these factors. Some of the observed overrepresentation seems to be a function of discriminatory attitudes and practices on the part of reporting sources with respect to minority groups. It is possible, however, that the higher reporting rate for nonwhites reflects also a real, higher incidence rate of child abuse among ethnic minority groups. Such a higher incidence rate among nonwhites is not unexpected in view of the higher incidence among them of socioeconomic deprivation, fatherless homes, and large families, all of which were found in the present study to be strongly associated with child abuse. Finally, since different ethnic groups may differ in child-rearing practices, the possibility cannot be ruled out that such differences between whites and nonwhites could be a contributing factor to the observed differences in reporting rates. Ethnically linked differences in using physical force in child-rearing may reflect the violence experienced by nonwhite minorities over many generations in American society.

Religion. The religious distribution of the 1967 sample cohort corresponded rather closely to the religious distribution of the United States population as reported in 1957 by the Bureau of the Census. Sixty-two percent of the sample cohort were Protestants and other non-Roman Catholic Christians, 25.5 percent Roman Catholics, 0.7 percent Jewish, 1.8 percent other religions, and the affiliation was unknown for 10.1 percent. The approximate religious distribution of the entire population is as follows: Protestants and other non-Roman Catholic Christians, 66 percent; Roman Catholics, 26 percent; Jewish, 3 percent; other religions, 1.5 percent; none or not reported, 3.5 percent.

Past and Present Functioning. Several items of the comprehensive level of the 1967 survey explored the past and present functioning of the abused children in the sample cohort. This exploration indicated that 29 percent of the children revealed deviations in social interaction and general functioning during the year preceding the abusive incident, nearly 14 percent suffered from deviations in physical functioning during that same time span, and nearly 8 percent revealed deviations in intellectual functioning. Among the school-aged children, over 13 percent attended special classes for retarded children or were in grades below their age level. Nearly 3 percent of the school-aged children had never attended school. Nearly 10 percent of children in the sample cohort had lived with foster families sometime during their lives prior to the incident, and over 3 percent had lived in child-care or correctional institutions. Over 5 percent had appeared before Juvenile Courts on other than traffic offenses.

Taken together, the several items exploring past and present functioning of the abused children in the sample cohort suggest a level of deviance in excess of the level of any group of children selected at random from the population at large. This impression is also supported by an overall rating on the item "persistent behavioral atypicality." This item was checked positively for nearly one quarter of the sample cohort.

Previous Abuse. At least half the children of the sample cohort had been victims of physical abuse prior to the incident reported in 1967. Since this item was checked as "unknown" for nearly one quarter of the sample cohort, it is quite likely that over 60 percent of the children had a history of prior abuse. Data for the 1967 and 1968 study cohorts suggest the same proportion of prior abuse. It thus seems that physical abuse of children is more often than not an indication of a prevailing pattern of caretaker-child interaction in a given home rather than of an isolated incident. This impression is supported also by data on involvement in previous abuse by parents, siblings, and other perpetrators, to be reported below.

Family Structure. Over 29 percent of children of the sample cohort lived in homes without a father or father substitute. The child's own father was living in the home in 46 percent of the cases, and in nearly one fifth of the cases a stepfather lived in the child's home. Over 2 percent of the children lived in foster homes, and 0.3 percent lived with adoptive parents. The child's own mother was not living in his home in over 12 percent of the sample cohort.

Ten percent of mothers of children in the sample cohort were single; nearly one fifth were separated, divorced, deserted, or widowed; and over two thirds were living with a spouse. Of the fathers or father substitutes over 2 percent were separated, divorced, deserted, or widowed, and over 96 percent were living with a spouse.

Examining family structure separately for different ethnic groups of the sample cohort reveals that over 37 percent of Negro children and 42 percent of Puerto Rican children, as against less than 20 percent of white children, lived in homes without fathers or substitutes. Their own fathers were living in the homes of 36 percent of the Negro children, 44 percent of the Puerto Rican children and 56 percent of the white children.

Fifteen percent of Negro and over 19 percent of Puerto Rican mothers were single as against 3.5 percent of the white mothers. About 22 percent of Negro and Puerto Rican mothers, as against 15.5 percent of white mothers, were separated, divorced, deserted, or widowed. About 60 percent of Negro and Puerto Rican mothers, as against 79 percent of white mothers, were living with a spouse.

The foregoing findings on family structure of the sample cohort suggest an association between physical abuse of children and deviance from normative nuclear family structure, which seems especially strong for nonwhite children.

Age of Parents. The age distribution of the parents or parent substitutes from the sample cohort is shown in Table 20. The table is based on 1,356 mothers or substitutes and 975 fathers or substitutes, since 24 children had no mothers in the home and 405 children had no fathers.

Table 20. Age Distribution of Parent or Parent Substitutes

Age	Mothers[a]		Fathers[b]	
---	Percent	Cum. Percent	Percent	Cum. Percent
Under 20	9.29	9.29	2.77	2.77
20 to under 25	26.18	35.47	16.41	19.18
25 to under 30	20.94	56.41	17.44	36.62
30 to under 40	24.12	80.53	32.00	68.62
40 to under 50	7.60	88.13	14.05	82.67
50 to under 60	1.70	89.83	4.41	87.08
60 to under 70	0.44	90.27	0.72	87.80
Over 70	0.37	90.64	0.10	87.90
Unknown	9.37	100.01	12.10	100.00

[a] Base = 1,356.   [b] Base = 975.

This age distribution does not support the observation of many earlier studies of physically abused children and their families, according to which the parents tend to be extremely young.

Number of Children. The distribution of sample cohort families by number of children is shown in Table 21 together with

Table 21. Number of Children

| Number of Children | Percent of Sample Cohort | | | | Percent of U.S. Families with Children under 18[a] |
	Total Cohort	White Families	Negro Families	Puerto Rican Families	
1	17.2	22.0	13.7	8.6	31.76
2	21.3	22.8	19.4	23.7	29.69
3	19.3	20.0	20.2	17.2	18.94
4 or more	37.4	30.6	42.3	48.5	19.60
Unknown	4.7	4.7	4.4	2.2	
	N = 1380	N = 536	N = 630	N = 93	N = 28,592,000

[a] Statistical Abstract of the United States (1968), p. 38.

figures for all families with children under 18 in the United States in 1967. The table reveals that the proportion of families with four or more children was nearly twice as high for the sample cohort as a whole as for all families in the U.S. population, and the proportion of small families was much larger in the U.S. population than in the sample cohort. The table also shows that the proportion of larger families among nonwhite families of the sample cohort was significantly higher than among white families.

Educational and Occupational Status of Parents. The educational level of the parents or substitutes of the sample cohort was fairly low. Of the mothers, 0.4 percent had never gone to school, 24 percent had less than 9 years of schooling, 40.6 percent had 9 to under 12 years, 16.7 percent were high school graduates, 4.4 percent had some college education, and 0.4 percent were college graduates. Of the fathers, 0.3 percent had no schooling, 23.5 percent had less than 9 years, 31.7 percent had between 9 and 12 years, 16.8 percent were high school graduates, 6.4 percent had some college education, 1.3 percent were college graduates, and 0.9 percent had graduate degrees. The educational level was unknown for 13.5 percent of the mothers and 19.1 percent of the fathers. The educational level of parents of nonwhite children as a group was lower than that of parents of white children.

The occupational status of parents of the sample cohort children corresponded to their low educational status. Thirty-nine percent of the mothers were in the labor force. Of these, 31.2 percent were in service occupations, 16.4 percent did clerical work, 11.2 percent were operatives, 6.3 percent were private household workers, 3.2 percent were laborers, 4.7 percent were sales workers, 6 percent were professional, technical, or managerial workers, 0.9 percent were foremen, and 0.4 percent were students. The occupational status was unknown for 19 percent. Of the fathers, 24.5 percent were laborers, 21.5 percent were operatives, 15.8 percent were craftsmen or foremen, 10.8 percent were service workers, 4.3 percent were electrical workers, 6.6 percent were professional, technical, or managerial workers, 2.4 percent were sales workers, and 0.5 percent were students. The occupation was unknown for 13.5 percent.

Only 52.5 percent of the fathers of sample cohort children were employed throughout the year. Twenty-seven percent of the fathers were unemployed part of the time, 5.3 percent were unemployed for the entire year. This item was not known for 15.1 percent of the fathers. Of the working mothers, only 30.1 percent were employed throughout the year. At the time of the abuse incident, 11.8 percent of the fathers were actually unemployed, a rate about three times as high as the nationwide unemployment rate. Employment rates were lower and unemployment rates higher for nonwhite fathers.

Family Income. The income of the families in the sample cohort was very low compared to the income of all families in the United States. Table 22 shows the distribution of income for

Table 22. Family Income — 1967

		Percent of Sample Cohort			Percent of
	All			*Puerto*	*all U.S.*
Income in $	*Families*	*White*	*Negro*	*Rican*	*Families*[a]
Under 3,000	22.3	17.7	24.8	34.5	12.5
3,000 to 4,999	26.1	21.9	28.6	41.9	12.8
5,000 to 6,999	16.2	18.5	14.1	9.7	16.1
7,000 to 9,999	12.7	15.9	11.7	5.4	24.3
10,000 to 14,999	2.6	3.1	1.9	1.1	22.4
15,000 and over	0.4	0.9	0.2	0.0	12.0
Unknown	19.8	22.2	18.6	7.5	0.0
	N = 1380	N = 536	N = 630	N = 93	N = 49,834,000

[a] *Consumer Income,* Bureau of the Census, Current Population Reports, Series P-60 (April 1969), No. 59.

all sample cohort families, for white, Negro, and Puerto Rican families in the sample and for all families in the United States.

Public Assistance Status. A further indication of the low socio-economic status of the sample cohort families is the fact that at the time of the abusive incident 34.1 percent of all families were receiving AFDC grants and 3.1 percent were receiving other public-assistance grants. Thus nearly 4 in 10 families were on public assistance. Altogether, nearly 60 percent of the families had received aid from public assistance agencies during or prior to the study year.

Analysis of the public assistance status of families from different ethnic groups in the sample cohort reveals that 46.3 percent Negro families and 61.3 percent Puerto Rican families, as against 17.6 percent white families, were recipients of AFDC grants at the time of the abuse report; and over 66 percent Negro families, 70 percent Puerto Rican families, and 40.3 percent white families had received some form of public assistance during or prior to the study year.

Housing and Mobility. Nearly 12 percent of sample cohort families lived in public housing, 51.4 percent in privately rented apartments, 18.3 percent in privately rented homes and only 13.1 percent in their own homes; nearly one percent lived in trailers. Over 14 percent of the families shared their living quarters with another family unit.

The families of the sample cohort revealed a high degree of mobility in living quarters. Nearly half the families had been living one year or less in the homes they occupied at the time of the incident, about one quarter had been in their homes from 1 to 3 years, and about 27 percent had lived in their homes for 3 years or longer.

Past and Present Functioning of Parents. The study explored selected aspects concerning the background and functioning of parents or parent substitutes of sample cohort children. This exploration revealed that 6.6 percent of the mothers had been hospitalized in mental hospitals at some time prior to the abuse incident, 6.4 percent had appeared in juvenile courts, 8.5 percent had experienced some type of foster care, and 4.7 percent had a criminal record; 10.4 percent of the mothers were judged deviant in intellectual functioning. During the year preceding the abuse incident, 10.5 percent of the mothers experienced medical problems, and 42.7 percent were judged deviant in social and behavioral functioning. The corresponding rates for the fathers are: hospitalization for mental illness, 4.4 percent; juvenile court involvement, 7.0 percent; foster care, 7.1 percent; criminal record, 15.6 percent; intellectual deviance, 6.9 percent; medical problems during year preceding the incident, 9.6 percent; social and behavioral deviance during the last year, 45.4 percent.

Past Involvement in Abuse of Parents. It has been mentioned earlier, when describing the children of the study and sample cohorts, that a large proportion of them were abused more than once, and that this seemed to reflect a child-rearing pattern that utilizes force toward children for disciplinary objectives. The findings on repeated abuse of children are matched by the following findings on repeated involvement in abuse incidents of parents. This item of the schedule had a high rate of "unknown" responses, but it is known that at least 14.1 percent of mothers and 7.0 percent of fathers had been victims of abuse in their childhood, and at least 31.6 percent of mothers and 39.9 percent of fathers had been perpetrators of abuse in the past. It is also known that in 27.1 percent of the sample cohort families, siblings of the currently abused child had been victims of physical child abuse prior to the present incident. Furthermore, 41 children or 0.7 percent of the 1967 study cohort and 78 children or 1.2 percent of the 1968 study cohort were reported to have been abused more than once during one study year.[4]

Summary of Family Circumstances. Summarizing the characteristics of the families in the sample cohort as reflected by indicators of educational achievement, occupational position and status, income and assistance status, number of children, and housing, one sees that families with a low socioeconomic background were overrepresented in this cohort, especially among the nonwhite families. Notable trends concerning family structure seem to be a high proportion of households headed by females, an even higher proportion of absence of biological father, and a higher than average birthrate.

Data concerning the past and recent history of parents in the sample cohort suggest a level of deviance in areas of psychosocial functioning which exceeds deviance levels in the general population. In this connection, it should be noted that items on parental functioning were checked "unknown" for many parents, and the rates obtained represent, therefore, only the minimum level. On the other hand, it should also be noted that some of these items

4. It should be noted that children who were reported abused more than once during one study year are counted only once in their respective study cohort, since the unit of count for the cohorts is a child abused during a study year, irrespective of the number of incidents in which he was involved.

are quite crude, and the response to them may not be sufficiently reliable.

Perpetrators. Since more than one child or more than one perpetrator is involved in many incidents of abuse, the same perpetrator may be involved in incidents with different children, and the same child may be abused by different perpetrators on different occasions, the numbers of children and the numbers of perpetrators may differ during any given time period. These sources of noncorrespondence between numbers of children, numbers of perpetrators, and numbers of incidents, as well as the noncorrespondence between numbers of children and numbers of families, should be kept in mind. The unit of analysis in the present discussion is usually one abused child or one "child incident," which is one incident affecting one child.

A total of 5,695 different perpetrators were involved in or suspected of abusing the 5,993 children of the 1967 study cohort; 6,508 perpetrators were involved in or suspected of abusing the 6,617 children of the 1968 study cohort; and 1,327 perpetrators were involved in or suspected of abusing the 1,380 children of the sample cohort. The quantitative relations between children and perpetrators are shown in Tables 23 and 24.

Table 23. Proportion of Incidents Involving One or More Perpetrators Respectively

	Proportion of Child Incidents		
	Study Cohorts		Sample Cohort
	1967	1968[a]	1967
Number of Perpetrators	N = 5993	N = 6617	N = 1380
1	95.24	87.44	92.02
2	4.73	6.41	7.11
3	0.03	0.58	—
Unknown	—	5.63	0.87
Total	100.00	100.06	100.00

[a] Estimate.

Table 24. Proportion of Incidents Involving One or More Children
Respectively

| | Proportion of Child Incidents | | |
| | Study Cohorts | | Sample Cohort |
Number of Children per Incident	1967 N = 5993	1968 N = 6617	1967 N = 1380
1	61.1	65.3	83.8
2	8.9	7.6	8.4
3	3.1	1.9	3.7
4	1.8	1.0	0.7
5	0.6	0.9	1.1
6	0.3	0.1	0.0
7 or more	0.2	0.2	0.0
Unknown	23.9	23.0	2.4
Total	99.9	100.0	100.1

In 47.6 percent of the sample cohort the child was abused by
his mother or mother substitute, in 39.2 percent by his father or
father substitute. Thus in 86.8 percent the perpetrator was a
parent or parent substitute with whom the child had been living.
In 12.1 percent the perpetrator was another relative, and in 1.1
percent the relationship of the perpetrator to the child was unknown. In 1 percent of the cases of the sample cohort a mother
or substitute was the second perpetrator, and in 5.7 percent
a father or substitute was second perpetrator. In 0.3 percent
another relative was second perpetrator.

Though in absolute numbers slightly more children in the
sample cohort were abused by mothers than by fathers, one must
remember that 29.5 percent of the children were living in fatherless homes. Fathers or substitutes were involved as perpetrators
in nearly two thirds of the incidents occurring in homes that did
have fathers or father substitutes, and mothers or substitutes
were involved in slightly fewer than one half the incidents occurring in homes that did have a mother or mother substitute.
Thus the involvement rate of fathers was actually higher than of
mothers. It is also noteworthy that about one third of the fathers

or substitutes who were involved as perpetrators were not biological fathers but stepfathers.

Additional analysis of the perpetrator-child relationship shows
that 71.1 percent of the children in the sample cohort were
abused by a biological parent, 0.4 percent by an adoptive parent,
13.6 percent by a step-parent, 2 percent by a foster parent, 0.7
percent by a sibling, 4.3 percent by other relatives, 6.5 percent
by unrelated perpetrators, and 1.4 percent by perpetrators
whose relationship to the victim was unknown.

Fifty-one percent of the children were abused by female perpetrators, 47.8 percent by male perpetrators, and 1.2 percent by
perpetrators whose sex was unknown.

Since about 87 percent of the children of the sample cohort
were abused by their parent or parent substitutes, the description
of parents as a group provides also an approximate picture of
the perpetrators. Briefly, then, perpetrators tended to have little
education and a low socioeconomic status. About 61 percent
were members of minority groups, 56.8 percent had shown
deviations in social and behavioral functioning during the year
preceding the abuse incident, and about 12.3 percent had been
physically ill during that year. Nearly 11 percent showed deviations in intellectual functioning, 7.1 percent had been in mental
hospitals some time prior to the incident, 8.4 percent had been
before juvenile courts, and 7.9 percent had been in foster care.
Under 14 percent had a criminal record. About 11 percent had
been victims of abuse during their own childhood, and 52.5
percent had been perpetrators of abuse prior to the current
incident.

The identity of perpetrators in the sample cohort was clearly
established by court procedures in 20.1 percent of the incidents
and by other than court procedures in 45.1 percent. The identity
was suspected in 33.5 percent, and it was neither known nor
suspected in 1.3 percent.

In descriptions of perpetrators and their relationship to the children they abused, only data from the sample cohort were used, since data from the study cohorts are less complete. However, the trends revealed by data from the sample cohort do not differ markedly from those revealed by data available on the study cohorts.

The Incidents and the Circumstances Surrounding Them

Place and Time. Over 90 percent of the abuse incidents of the sample cohort occurred in the child's home, 2.5 percent occurred in the home of a perpetrator who was not a member of the child's family, 2 percent occurred in a public place, under one percent in a school or child-care facility, and nearly 2 percent in another locality; in nearly 3 percent the place of the incident was unknown. As can be expected, the hours before and after dinner time are the high-risk hours during the day. Nearly 18.7 percent of incidents occurred between 3 and 6 P.M., 19.6 percent between 6 and 9 P.M., and 9.3 percent occurred between 9 P.M. and midnight. The incidence rate during other three-hour periods varied from 1.4 percent to 8.7 percent. There were no marked differences in incidence rate between the seven days of the week and the twelve months of the year.

Types of Injuries. The types of injuries sustained by children of the sample cohort are shown in Table 25. This distribution is similar to the one reported for children of the nationwide study cohorts.

The tabulation of injuries is based on medical verification in 80.2 percent of the cases, and the reliability of the diagnoses is therefore quite satisfactory. The injuries were considered to be "not serious" in 53.3 percent. They were rated "serious, no permanent damage expected" in 36.5 percent, "serious with permanent damage" in 4.6 percent, and fatal in 3.4 percent. The degree of seriousness was medically verified in 78.9 percent of the cases. The ratings of seriousness take into consideration only

Table 25. Types of Injuries Sustained by Children in Current Abuse Incident

Injury	Percent of Children[a]
Bruises, welts	67.1
Abrasions, contusions, lacerations	32.3
Wounds, cuts, punctures	7.9
Burns, scalding	10.1
Bone fractures (excluding skull)	10.4
Sprains, dislocations	1.9
Skull fractures	3.7
Subdural hemorrhage or hematoma	4.6
Brain damage	1.5
Internal injuries	3.3
Poisoning	0.9
Malnutrition (deliberately inflicted)	4.2
Freezing, exposure	0.1
Other injuries	5.4
No apparent injuries	3.2
Type unknown	2.2

[a] The percentages in this table do not add up to 100 because many children sustained more than one injury. $N = 1380$.

the physical aspects of the injury and disregard possible emotional aspects. It is noteworthy, however, that 90 percent of the reported incidents were not expected to leave any lasting physical effects on the children, and that over half the incidents were not considered to be serious at all. Considering these findings, one must certainly question the view of many concerned professional and lay persons, according to which physical abuse of children constitutes a major cause of death and maiming of children throughout the nation.

As observed earlier in this discussion, bias was introduced in the study because of underreporting of fatalities of children which may have been caused by physical abuse. To compensate for this a press survey was conducted. During the six-month period from July to December 1967, a nationwide screening of daily papers in the U.S. and its territories yielded reports on 164 fatalities due to physical abuse of children. The checking of press reports against 134 official reports on fatalities from the 1967 study cohort revealed that about 90 percent of the fatalities known to the press had not entered the official reporting systems.

The yield of the press survey of fatalities for July to December 1967 was compared with the yield of a survey designed in the identical manner and conducted from July to December 1965. Surprisingly enough, the yield was identical: 164 fatalities.

As a further check on the incidence of fatalities due to physical child abuse, official homicide figures were examined. The National Center for Health Statistics of the U.S. Public Health Service reported that a total of 686 children under age 15 were victims of homicides during 1967.[5] Of the victims, 226 were under one year, 174 from one to 4 years, and 286 from 5 to under 15 years. These figures, it should be noted, include homicides by caretakers and noncaretakers of the victims and are, therefore, not an accurate count of fatalities due to child abuse. On the other hand, the figures cover only groups under age 15. Furthermore, some deaths which the Bureau classified as accidents may have involved components of intentional abuse. It does seem, therefore, that the number of deaths due to physical child abuse was higher than the 134 cases reported to the survey for 1967. The Bureau of Vital Statistics reported also that the homicide rate for infants increased between 1963 and 1967 from 5.0 to 6.4 deaths per 100,000 live births.

The relationship between severity of injury and age has already been mentioned. Injuries of children under age 3 were serious or fatal in 65 percent of the cases, and injuries of children over age 3 were serious in 35 percent of the cases only.

The severity of injuries was found to be related also to ethnicity. The injuries of white children were judged not serious in 61.6 percent and serious or fatal in 35.2 percent. The injuries of Negro and Puerto Rican children were judged not serious in 47.3

5. *Monthly Vital Statistics Report,* 17, No. 12 (May 25, 1969), p. 4.

percent and serious in 52.0 percent. The severity of injury was found not to be associated with the victim's sex, however.

Several less pronounced associational trends were revealed by data from the sample cohort concerning the severity of injuries sustained by abused children. Severe injuries were more likely to be inflicted by parents and other perpetrators under age 25 than by older ones. Severe injuries were more likely to be inflicted by women than by men and especially by single women. Parents who had appeared before juvenile courts and who experienced some form of foster care were more likely than other parents to inflict serious injury. Finally, injuries were more likely to be serious or fatal in families whose annual income was under $3,500.

The manner in which the injuries of children in the sample cohort were inflicted is shown in Table 26.

Table 26. Manner by Which Injuries Were Inflicted

Manner of Infliction	Percent[a]
Beating with hands	39.3
Beating with instruments	44.2
Kicking	4.0
Burning, scalding	9.1
Strangling, suffocating	1.2
Drowning	0.2
Stabbing, slashing	1.0
Poisoning	0.9
Deliberate neglect or exposure	3.8
Locking in or tying	1.7
Other manner	9.3
Manner unknown	13.1

[a] Percentages do not add up to 100 because several children were abused in more than one manner. N = 1380.

Different ethnic groups seem to prefer different methods in abusing children. Whites tend to use their bare hands without instruments to a larger extent than do nonwhites, and burning and scalding was used by Puerto Ricans to a far greater extent than by any other group. These different tendencies concerning the type of physical force used in interaction with children may be a contributory factor to the possibly higher incidence of physical child abuse among nonwhites, and to the higher rate of serious injury suffered by nonwhite children of the sample cohort.

Circumstances Surrounding Incidents. While, as already mentioned, nearly all incidents of abuse in the sample cohort took place in the child's own home, they usually occurred in the presence of several persons besides the victim and the perpetrator. Other children from the same household were on the scene in 62.2 percent of the cases, the mother or substitute in 25.9 percent, the father or substitute in 4.6 percent, other adult members of the household in 5.9 percent, children from outside the household in 3.4 percent, and adults from outside the household in 8.2 percent.

The injured child's health and welfare may depend to a considerable extent on actions taken subsequent to an abusive incident. Delay in obtaining help may have serious consequences. A set of items in the comprehensive study focused on this issue. It was learned that the perpetrators themselves initiated help for the victims in 21.2 percent of the incidents. In 35.7 percent of the incidents, members of the victim's household other than the perpetrator initiated help. Thus in 56.9 percent of the cases the child's own family acted to obtain help once they noticed the results of the abusive treatment. School or child-care personnel initiated help in 16.4 percent of the cases, and in 31.7 percent others, such as neighbors or visiting relatives, initiated help for the child. Occasionally help was initiated simultaneously by more than one source.

Table 27 shows the resources to which those initiating help turned in order to obtain care and protection for the abused children of the sample cohort.

Clearly, then, medical resources were the first choice for help,

Table 27. Resource First Contacted for Help Subsequent to Incident

Resource	Percentage N = 1380
Hospital or clinic	46.2
Private medical doctor	5.1
. . . .	. . .
Subtotal: Medical resources	51.3
. . . .	. . .
Police	29.4
Public social agency	15.2
Private social agency	1.0
Other	2.9
Unknown	0.1

the police were next, and social agencies were the third choice.

In 30.7 percent of the cases, fewer than 3 hours passed between the incident and the initial contact with the chosen source of help. In 15.1 percent it took from 3 to 12 hours, in 13.2 percent from 12 hours to one day, in 9.0 percent from one to 2 days, in 12.8 percent from 2 days to one week, in 4.6 percent from one week to one month, in 2.8 percent one month or more. The timing was unknown in 9.7 percent of the cases.

It is of some interest to compare Table 27 with Table 28,

Table 28. Official Sources Reporting Incidents

Source	Percentage N = 1380
Hospital or clinic	49.0
Private medical doctor	2.8
. . . .	. . .
Subtotal: Medical resources	51.8
. . . .	. . .
Police	23.2
Public social agency	7.9
Private social agency	0.1
School or child care facility	12.4
Public health nurse or V.N.S.	0.9
Other	1.7
Unknown	2.0

which shows the official reporting sources for the abusive incidents in the sample cohort.

As can be seen, private medical doctors were the initial source contacted for help in 5.1 percent of the cases, but they filed the official reports in only 2.8 percent of the cases. Although schools, for obvious reasons, were an active source for reporting incidents, they were not contacted at all as a source for help. The marked difference in the two tables concerning the police and public social agencies seems due to the fact that these agencies are in most states the legally established recipients of child-abuse reports, and therefore they would not be checked as "sources of reports."

Medical Treatment. The extent of medical treatment subsequent to the abusive incidents of the sample cohort is shown in Table 29.

Table 29. Medical Treatment Rendered to Children Subsequent to Incidents

Extent of Treatment	Percentage N = 1380
No medical treatment	23.7
One treatment contact only	27.8
More than one treatment contact outside hospital	7.1
Hospitalization up to 1 day	4.7
Hospitalization 2–7 days	10.6
Hospitalization 8–30 days	14.0
Hospitalization over 30 days	7.3
Other	1.0
Unknown	3.8

This table is another crude indicator of the degree of severity of physical abuse sustained by children of the sample cohort. The injuries of nearly 60 percent of the children did not seem to require hospitalization, and in nearly 25 percent no medical treatment seemed indicated. Of those requiring hospitalization, over 41.7 percent were discharged in less than one week. Hospitalization beyond one week was required by 21.3 percent of the children, and this group seems to represent the segment of severe injury of the child-abuse spectrum, which ranges from incidents without injury to incidents resulting in death.

Official Intervention Subsequent to Incidents of Abuse. While public and voluntary social welfare agencies were a third choice as an initial source for help following abusive incidents, they carried major responsibility in dealing with and caring for the abused children and their families later on. Social welfare agencies were involved to some extent in 86.9 percent of the cases in the sample cohort. Courts were involved in 45.8 percent, the police in 53.1 percent, and district or county attorneys in 19.1 percent.

Over 36 percent of children of the sample cohort were placed away from their families after the abuse incidents. In 15.4 percent of the cases, not only the victims but also siblings living in the same homes were placed away from their families. Placement away from the child's home was more likely to be used when injuries were serious and when children had been abused before. Homemaker service was made available to 2.2 percent of the families, and counseling services were made available to 71.9 percent.

The suspected perpetrators were indicted in 17.3 percent of the incidents. They were convicted in 13.1 percent and jailed in 7.2 percent. Court action was more likely to be taken when children were seriously or fatally injured.

A Typology of Child Abuse

Based on observations throughout the stages of this study, the conclusion was reached that physical abuse of children is not a uniform phenomenon with one set of causal factors, but a multidimensional phenomenon. Following Alfred J. Kahn's reasoning concerning the phenomenon of juvenile delinquency to which he refers as "delinquencies," [6] it seems necessary to view the phenomenon studied here as "child abuses," rather than as "child abuse." This change in terms suggests that the phenomenon, while uniform in symptoms, is nevertheless likely to be diverse in causation. Such a conceptualization may also help to avoid fruitless arguments between those who believe that child abuse is caused by the psychopathology of the perpetrators and those who see the phenomenon related primarily to cultural, social, and economic factors.

In order to explore the many possible contributing causal contexts that may precipitate incidents of physical abuse of children, a substudy was built into the comprehensive level of the nationwide survey. Social workers who completed study schedules were asked to prepare for each case a separate checklist of circumstances which may or may not have been present in any given case.[7] The list had been developed empirically on the basis of a content analysis of a pilot study conducted in California during 1966. The items were not designed to be mutually exclusive. Associations between two or more types were therefore expected in many incidents. Responses concerning the circumstances of abuse of the 1,380 cases of the sample cohort suggest the following observations concerning types of physical child abuse:

One major type involves incidents developing out of disciplinary action taken by caretakers who respond in uncontrolled anger to real or perceived misconduct of a child. Nearly 63 percent of the cases were checked as "immediate or delayed response to specific act of child," and nearly 73 percent were checked as "inadequately controlled anger of perpetrator." In this connection, it may be noted that in only 22.1 percent the item "misconduct of child by community standards" was

6. "Social Work and the Control of Delinquency: Theory and Strategy," *Social Work,* 10 (1965), 3–13.

7. See Appendix E.

checked. This seems to suggest that the standards for misconduct used by the perpetrators seem to be more severe than general community standards. It is important to keep in mind in connection with this type that the majority of sample cases came from families with a low socioeconomic and educational background. Studies of child-rearing patterns have found a strong association between low socioeconomic status and the use of physical means in disciplining children.[8] It has also been observed that the uninhibited acting out of aggressive impulses is more likely to occur in poor and working-class families than in middle-class families.

A second important type seems to involve incidents that derive from a general attitude of resentment and rejection on the part of the perpetrator toward a child. In these cases, not a specific act but the "whole person," or a specific quality in the person such as his sex, his looks, his capacities, the status, and the circumstances of his birth, is the object of rejection. In these cases, too, specific acts of the child may precipitate the acting out of the underlying attitude of rejection. The item "Resentment, rejection of child . . ." which tested the presence of this type was checked in 34.1 percent of the cases. This type was associated with "Repeated abuse of same child by perpetrator," and also "Battered child syndrome." These two items were checked in 47.6 percent and 13.6 percent respectively.

A third type is defined by the item "Persistent behavioral atypicality of child, e.g., hyperactivity, high annoyance poten-

8. See D. Miller and G. Swanson, *Inner Conflict and Defense* (New York, Holt, Rinehart & Winston, 1960). The following relationship was found in that study:

Social Class and Type of Discipline

Social Class	Types of Discipline		
	Non-Corporal-Psychological	*Mixed*	*Corporal*
Middle	76%	13%	11%
Working	12%	36%	52%

tial, etc." Cases checked positively on this item may be considered as child-initiated or child-provoked abuse. This item was checked in 24.5 percent of the cases. This type was found to be associated with "Misconduct of child," which was checked in over 22 percent of the cases.

A fourth type is physical abuse of a child developing out of a quarrel between his caretakers. The child may come to the aid of one parent, or he may just happen to be in the midst of a fight between the parents. Sometimes the child may even be the object of the fight. The item reflecting this type was checked in 11.3 percent of the cases. It was associated with "Alcoholic intoxication of perpetrator," which was checked in 12.9 percent of the cases.

A fifth type is physical abuse coinciding with a perpetrator's sexual attack on a child. This may occur as a result of frustration when the child rejects the advances of the perpetrator, or it may be part of perverse sexual interaction. This item was checked in 0.6 percent of the cases. It was found to be associated with the sixth type, "Sadistic gratification of the perpetrator," which was checked in 7.5 percent of the cases.

The seventh type may be referred to as sadism sublimated to the level of child-rearing ideology. The item was worded on the checklist: "Self-definition of perpetrator as stern, authoritative disciplinarian." This item may also have a strong cultural component. It was checked in 31 percent of the cases, and was associated with the first type.

Type 8 was called "Marked mental and/or emotional deviation of perpetrator." This type overlapped with several others. It was checked in 46.1 percent of the cases and was associated with "Mounting stress on perpetrator," which was checked in 59 percent of the cases.

Type 9 is the simultaneous occurrence of abuse and neglect. Contrary to the hypothesis of many investigators who consider abuse and neglect as mutually exclusive phenomena, this type was checked in 33.7 percent of the cases. It was associated with "Resentment, rejection . . ."

The "battered child syndrome" as described and defined by Dr. Kempe[9] constitutes Type 10. This item was checked in 13.6 percent of the cases. It was associated with "Resentment, rejection . . ."

"Alcoholic intoxication of the perpetrator at the time of the abusive act" constitutes Type 11. This item was checked as present in 12.9 percent of the cases and was associated with "Caretaker quarrel," and "Mother temporarily absent — perpetrator male."

A very important type is Number 12, "Mounting stress on perpetrator due to life circumstances." This item was checked as present in 59 percent of the cases and was associated with "Mental, emotional deviation of perpetrator."

Type 13 is an important "typical constellation" which frequently tends to precipitate physical abuse of a child: The mother or substitute is temporarily absent from the home, working or shopping, or for some other reason, and the child is left in the care of a boyfriend or some other male caretaker. This type was the context for the abuse in 17.2 percent of the cases in the sample cohort and seems to deserve special attention in any preventive effort. It was found to be associated with the categories "Physical and sexual abuse coincide," "Sadistic gratification of perpetrator," and "Alcoholic intoxication."

The last type, 14, is similar to 13 but quantitatively much less important as a typical context for child abuse. It is the temporary absence of the mother or substitute during which the child is cared for and abused by a female babysitter. This item was checked in 2.7 percent of the cases.

9. Kempe et al., "The Battered Child Syndrome," *Journal of the American Medical Association,* 181 (1962), 17–24.

The foregoing typology is quite crude and will require further exploration and testing. However, it may be of interest to note that in the current study, this typology seems to have successfully covered most of the circumstances of abuse observed by social workers who completed study schedules. This is reflected in the fact that a residual item — "other circumstances" — was checked only in 2.7 percent of the cases.

It should also be noted that the positive checks on the items of this typology represent the minimal level for each item, since there were responses of "unknown" on every one of the items.

Factor Analysis. Data underlying the foregoing empirically derived typology were subjected to a factor analysis. The final results of this analysis, shown in Table 30, suggest that the typology can be reduced to the following underlying seven factors of legally reported physical child abuse:

1. Psychological rejection: This factor is reflected in high loadings on "Resentment, rejection of child," "Repeated abuse," and "Battered child." The factor shows also moderately high loadings on "Sadistic gratification" and "Abuse and neglect coincide."
2. Angry and uncontrolled disciplinary response: This factor shows high loadings on "Perpetrator response to child's act," "Inadequately controlled anger," and "Perpetrator stern disciplinarian."
3. Male babysitter abuse: This factor consists of high loadings on "Mother temporarily absent — male perpetrator," "Physical and sexual abuse coincide," "Sadistic gratification," and "Alcoholic intoxication."
4. Personality deviance and reality stress: This factor's high loadings are "Mental and/or emotional deviation of perpetrator" and "Mounting stress on perpetrator."
5. Child-originated abuse: This factor results from high loadings on "Misconduct of child" and "Behavioral atypicality of child."

Table 30. Factor Analysis of Circumstances of Child Abuse: Rotated Factor Loadings (Orthogonal Varimax, Rotation by Variable)

Type of Circumstances	Factors							Communality
	1	2	3	4	5	6	7	
1. Perpetrator response to child's act	-.069	.739[a]	-.100	-.032	.253	.013	.208	.670
2. Misconduct of child	-.266	.235	.051	-.122	.714[a]	-.074	.128	.676
3. Inadequately controlled anger	-.050	.805[a]	-.170	.115	-.009	-.119	-.129	.724
4. Resentment, rejection of child	.620[a]	.003	-.092	.192	-.083	-.022	-.060	.440
5. Repeated abuse of same child	.729[a]	.200	.084	.059	.039	-.135	.058	.605
6. Persistent behavioral atypicality	.071	.069	-.007	.053	.797[a]	-.048	.044	.652
7. Physical abuse and sexual attack coincide	.022	-.235	.673[a]	-.060	.165	.074	-.143	.565
8. Abuse resulting from caretaker quarrel	-.004	-.068	.057	-.020	-.078	-.048	-.880[a]	.791
9. Battered child syndrome	.675[a]	-.148	.051	-.110	-.029	-.015	.027	.494
10. Abuse and neglect coincide	.431[b]	-.328	.068	.340	.026	.050	-.001	.417
11. Mental, emotional deviation of perpetrator	.306	.019	.188	.675[a]	-.256	.025	-.004	.651
12. Sadistic gratification of perpetrator	.445[b]	.017	.546[a]	.135	-.110	.251	-.080	.595
13. Alcoholic intoxication of perpetrator	-.036	.039	.493[a]	.148	-.103	.022	-.499[a]	.529
14. Perpetrator stern disciplinarian	.212	.522[a]	.369	-.178	.167	.098	.042	.525
15. Mounting stress on perpetrator	-.031	.003	-.121	.813[a]	.124	-.062	-.040	.697
16. Mother absent; perpetrator male	-.274	.031	.554[a]	-.087	-.389	-.365	.267	.746
17. Mother absent; perpetrator female	-.143	-.052	.108	-.051	-.105	.899[a]	.059	.861
Sums of Squares	2.075	1.762	1.566	1.403	1.547	1.071	1.214	10.638

[a] high loadings
[b] moderately high loadings

6. Female babysitter abuse: This factor appears to be independent, having high loadings only on "Mother temporarily absent — female perpetrator."

7. Caretaker quarrel: This factor consists of high loadings on "Abuse resulting from quarrel between caretakers" and "Alcoholic intoxication of perpetrator."

These seven factors reflect the existence of strong associations between certain sets of empirically observed circumstances of physical child abuse and constitute, therefore, a more refined typology of child abuses inflicted upon the children of the sample cohort. Since the 1967 sample cohort was selected to be representative, within certain limitations, of the entire 1967 study cohort, and since the 1968 study cohort appears to be similar in many relevant dimensions to the 1967 study cohort, it seems appropriate to suggest that this refined typology is a valid representation not only of the sample cohort, but also of the two study cohorts. Furthermore, it may not be too far-fetched an hypothesis to suggest that this refined typology provides a basis for predicting the nature and proportional distribution of future cohorts of physically abused children reported under currently existing, legally established reporting mechanisms of the states.

In a certain sense, the seven factors of the spectrum of legally reported physical abuse of children summarize the findings of the nationwide surveys by reducing them into a concentrated paradigm that reflects the underlying structure of the phenomenon under study. A more comprehensive conceptual summation of these findings, and a set of recommendations derived from them, are the subject of the final chapter.

Chapter Six

*A Conceptual Framework
and Recommendations*

The studies reported in preceding chapters were undertaken in order to narrow existing gaps in systematic knowledge concerning the nature and scope of physical abuse of children in the United States. They were conducted at a time when professional groups, communications media, and the general public manifested considerable interest in this subject, and when diverse opinions concerning it were publicized widely, often on the basis of insufficient factual data. Frequently, expressions of opinion followed the discovery of a particularly tragic incident of child abuse, and under its emotional impact.

To gain understanding of physical abuse of children as a phenomenon in American society it seems necessary to overcome the emotional impact of specific incidents, to go beyond the level of clinical diagnosis of individual cases, and to examine trends revealed by data on large cohorts of cases against the background of broader social and cultural forces. To conduct such an examination was the objective of the nationwide studies. The following observations suggest a conceptual framework derived from substantive findings of these studies. Based on this framework, several measures to reduce the incidence of physical child abuse in the United States are recommended.

A key element to understanding physical abuse of children in the United States seems to be that the context of child-rearing does not exclude the use of physical force toward children by parents and others responsible for their socialization. Rather, American culture encourages in subtle, and at times not so subtle, ways the use of "a certain measure" of physical force in rearing children in order to modify their inherently nonsocial inclinations. This cultural tendency can be noted in child-rearing practices of most segments of American society. It is supported in various ways by communications disseminated by the press, radio, and television, and by popular and professional publications.

Approval of a certain measure of physical force as a legitimate and appropriate educational and socializing agent seems thus endemic to American culture. Yet differences do exist between various segments of American society concerning the quantity and quality of physical force in child-rearing of which they approve, and which they actually practice. Thus, for instance, families of low socioeconomic and educational status tend to use corporal punishment to a far greater extent than do middle-class families. Also, different ethnic groups, because of differences in their history, experiences, and specific cultural traditions, seem to hold different views and seem to have evolved different practices concerning the use of physical force in child-rearing.

Although excessive use of physical force against children is considered abusive and is usually rejected in American tradition, practice, and law, no clear-cut criteria exist, nor would they be feasible, concerning the specific point beyond which the quantity and quality of physical force used against a child is to be considered excessive. The determination of this elusive point is left to the discretion of parents, other caretakers, professional personnel, health, education and welfare agencies, the police, and the courts. Implied in this ambiguous situation is the following question: What kind of forces singly, or in various combinations, result at certain times in culturally unacceptable "excessive" or "extreme" use of physical force against children on the part of caretakers? In other words, why and under what conditions do some persons go beyond a culturally sanctioned level of physical violence against children? Findings from the nationwide surveys suggest the following set of forces:

1. environmental chance factors;
2. environmental stress factors;
3. deviance or pathology in areas of physical, social, intellectual, and emotional functioning on the part of caretakers and/or the abused children themselves;
4. disturbed intrafamily relationships involving conflicts between spouses and/or rejection of individual children;
5. combinations between these sets of forces.

Judging by these forces, one concludes that the phenomenon of physical abuse of children should be viewed as multidimensional rather than uniform with one set of causal factors. Its basic dimension upon which all other factors are superimposed is the general, culturally determined permissive attitude toward the use of a measure of physical force in caretaker-child interaction, and the related absence of clear-cut legal prohibitions and sanctions against this particular form of interpersonal violence. A second dimension is determined by specific child-rearing traditions and practices of different social classes and ethnic and nationality groups, and the different attitudes of these groups toward physical force as an acceptable measure for the achievement of child-rearing objectives. A third dimension is determined by environmental chance circumstances, which may transform an otherwise acceptable disciplinary measure into an unacceptable outcome. A fourth dimension is the broad range of environmental stress factors which may weaken a person's psychological mechanisms of self-control, and may contribute thus to the uninhibited discharge of aggressive and destructive impulses toward physically powerless children, perceived to be causes of stress for real or imaginary reasons. The final dimension is the various forms of deviance in physical, social, intellectual, and emotional functioning of caretakers and/or children in their care, as well as of entire family units to which they belong.

The following substantive findings from the nationwide studies support the conceptual framework presented here. Culturally determined, permissive attitudes toward the use of physical force against children, and tolerant attitudes toward the perpetrators of such acts, were brought out most convincingly in the opinions expressed by a majority of respondents to the public opinion survey. Next, a majority of nearly 13,000 abusive incidents reported through legal channels during 1967 and 1968 resulted from more or less acceptable disciplinary measures taken by caretakers in angry response to actual or perceived misconduct of children in their care. Furthermore, a large majority of families involved in these reported incidents of abuse belonged to socioeconomically deprived segments of the population whose income and educational and occupational status were very low. Moreover, families from ethnic minority groups were overrepresented in the sample and study cohorts. Environmental chance factors were often found to have been decisive in transforming acceptable disciplinary measures into incidents of physical abuse resulting in injury, and a vast array of environmental stress situations were precipitating elements in a large proportion of the incidents. Finally, a higher than normal proportion of abused children, their abusers, and their families revealed a wide range of deviance and pathology in areas of physical, social, intellectual, and emotional functioning.

Before presenting a set of recommendations based on this conceptual framework, several more specific comments concerning selected substantive findings seem indicated.

Physical abuse of children does not seem to be a "major killer and maimer" of children as it was claimed to be in sensational publicity in the mass media of communication. Such exaggerated claims reflect an emotional response to this destructive phenomenon which, understandably, touches sensitive spots with nearly every adult, since many adults may themselves, at times, be subject to aggressive impulses toward children in their care. In spite of its strong emotional impact, and the tragic aspects of every single incident, the phenomenon of child abuse needs to be put into a more balanced perspective. Its true incidence rate has not been uncovered by the nationwide surveys. It seems, nevertheless, that the scope of physical abuse of children resulting in serious injury does not constitute a major social problem, at least in comparison with several more widespread and more serious social problems that undermine the developmental opportunities of many millions of children in American society, such as poverty, racial discrimination, malnutrition, and inadequate provisions for medical care and education.

Reporting levels and rates of physical child abuse did increase in several states from 1967 to 1968, while they decreased in several others. A net increase of about 10 percent occurred during this period throughout the United States. Increases in reporting rates have been interpreted by communications media and other sources as evidence of an increase in real incidence rates. Analysis of reporting patterns, however, does not support such an interpretation. Intrastate changes over time and interstate differences in levels and rates of reporting were found to be associated with differences in legal and administrative provisions and differences in professional concern and actions. They are therefore unlikely to reflect differences and changes in real incidence rates, and claims concerning increases or decreases of real incidence rates are based on insufficient and unreliable evidence.

Although the real incidence rate of all physical child abuse remains unknown in spite of reporting legislation, cohorts of officially reported incidents are likely to be a more adequate representation of the severe-injury segment of the physical child-abuse spectrum than of lesser or no-injury segments, since severity of injury is an important criterion in reporting. If, then, the 6,000 to 7,000 incidents that are reported annually through official channels are, as a group, an approximate representation of the severe segment of the nationwide abuse spectrum, then the physical consequences of child abuse do not seem to be very serious in the aggregate. This conclusion is based on data concerning the types and severity of injuries sustained by children of the 1967 and 1968 study cohorts. Over half these children suffered only minor injuries, and the classical "battered child syndrome" was found to be a relatively infrequent occurrence. Even if allowance is made for underreporting, especially of fatalities, physical abuse cannot be considered a major cause of mortality and morbidity of children in the United States.

Turning now to an epidemiologic perspective, it should be noted that physical abuse of children, and especially more serious incidents, were found to be overconcentrated among the poor and among nonwhite minorities, and thus seem to be one aspect of the style of life associated with poverty and the ghetto. While it may be valid to argue, on the basis of much evidence, that the poor and nonwhites are more likely to be reported for anything they do or fail to do, and that their overrepresentation in cohorts of reported child abuse may be in part a function of this kind of reporting bias, it must not be overlooked, nevertheless, that life in poverty and in the ghettos generates stressful experiences, which are likely to become precipitating factors of child abuse.

The poor and members of ethnic minorities are subject to the same conditions that may cause abusive behavior toward children in all other groups of the population. In addition, however, these people must experience the special environmental stresses and strains associated with socioeconomic deprivation and discrimination. Moreover, they have fewer alternatives and escapes than the nonpoor for dealing with aggressive impulses toward their children. Finally, there is an additional factor, the tendency toward more direct, less inhibited, expression and discharge of aggressive impulses, a tendency learned apparently through lower-class and ghetto socialization, which differ in this respect from middle-class mores and socialization.

Of considerable interest in terms of the forces contributing to child abuse are findings concerning the troubled past history of many abused children, their parents and perpetrators, and the relatively high rates of deviance in areas of bio-psycho-social functioning of children and adults involved in abuse incidents. In many instances manifestations of such deviance were observed during the year preceding the reported incident. Deviance in functioning of individuals was matched by high rates of deviance in family structure reflected in a high proportion of female-headed households and households from which the biological fathers of abused children were absent. In terms of family structure it is also worth noting that, as a group, families of physically abused children tend to have more children than other American families with children under age 18.

The age distribution of abused children and their parents was found to be less skewed toward younger age groups than had been thought on the basis of earlier, mainly hospital-based, studies. This difference in findings seems due to the fact that younger children tend to be more severely injured when abused and are, therefore, overrepresented among hospitalized abused children. More boys than girls seem to be subjected to physical abuse, yet girls seem to outnumber boys among adolescent abused children.

Although more mothers than fathers are reported as perpetrators of abuse, the involvement rate in incidents of child abuse is higher for fathers and stepfathers than for mothers. This important relationship is unraveled when account is taken of the fact that nearly 30 percent of reported abuse incidents occur in female-headed households. Altogether, nearly 87 percent of perpetrators are parents or parent substitutes.

Mention should be made of observations which support the hypotheses that some children play a contributive role in their own abuse, since their behavior seems to be more provocative and irritating to caretakers than the behavior of other children. Such atypical behavior may derive from constitutional or congenital factors, from environmental experiences, or from both.

Many children in the study had been abused on previous occasions, and siblings of many abused children were abused on the same or on previous occasions. Many perpetrators were involved in incidents of abuse on previous occasions, and many had been victims of abuse during their childhood. The high rate of recidivism reflected in these findings indicates that the use of physical force tends to be patterned into child-rearing practices and is usually not an isolated incident.

Circumstances precipitating incidents of abuse are quite diverse, yet underlying this diversity there seems to be a rather simple structure. A factor analysis of the circumstances of 1,380 abusive incidents of the sample cohort resulted in the following refined typology of circumstances of child abuse:

   a. Psychological rejection leading to repeated abuse and battering;
   b. Disciplinary measures taken in uncontrolled anger;
   c. Male babysitter acting out sadistic and sexual impulses in the mother's temporary absence, at times under the influence of alcohol;
   d. Mentally or emotionally disturbed caretaker acting under mounting environmental stress;

e. Misconduct and persistent behavioral atypicality of a child leading to his own abuse;

f. Female babysitter abusing child during mother's temporary absence;

g. Quarrel between caretakers, at times under the influence of alcohol.

Recommendations

Measures aimed at the prevention or the gradual reduction of the incidence and prevalence of specified social phenomena cannot be expected to achieve their purpose unless they are designed and executed in a manner that assures intervention on the causal level. Applying a public health model of preventive intervention to the phenomenon of physical abuse of children and proceeding on the conceptualization of its etiology, which has been presented above, I suggest the following measures:

1. Since culturally determined permissive attitudes toward the use of physical force in child-rearing seem to constitute the common core of all physical abuse of children in American society, systematic educational efforts aimed at gradually changing this particular aspect of the prevailing child-rearing philosophy, and developing clear-cut cultural prohibitions and legal sanctions against the use of physical force as a means for rearing children, are likely to produce over time the strongest possible reduction of the incidence and prevalence of physical abuse of children.

What is suggested here is, perhaps, a revolutionary change not only in the child-rearing philosophy and practices of American society but also in its underlying value system. Such a thorough change cannot be expected to occur overnight on the basis of a formal decision by governmental authority. What would be required is an extended, consistent effort in that direction which must eventually lead to a series of changes in our system of values and in the entire societal fabric.

It is important to keep in mind in this context that educational philosophies tend to reflect a social order and are not its primary shapers. Education tends to recreate a society in its existing image, or to maintain its relative status quo, but it rarely if ever creates new social structures. Violence against children in rearing them may thus be a functional aspect of socialization into a highly competitive and often violent society, one that puts a premium on the uninhibited pursuit of self-interest and that does not put into practice the philosophy of human cooperativeness which it preaches on ceremonial occasions and which is upheld in its ideological expressions and symbols. The elimination of violence from American child-rearing philosophy and practice seems therefore to depend on changes in social philosophy and social reality toward less competition and more human cooperativeness, mutual caring, and responsibility.[1]

The foregoing considerations suggest that a close connection may indeed exist between culturally acceptable violence against children and culturally unacceptable violence among adults and among various groups in American society. These considerations also suggest that to the extent that American society may succeed in reducing the amount of violence and abuse which it inflicts collectively on children in the course of their socialization, it may reduce the amount of violence in interpersonal and intergroup relations among adults in this country, and perhaps even in international relations on a global scale.

If physical force could gradually be eliminated as a mode of legitimate interaction between caretakers and children, some other more constructive modes of interaction would have to replace it. Children who were exposed to more constructive relationship patterns would be likely to learn from this experience and to carry it over into their adult relationships. They would no longer be exposed, as they are now, to conflicting signals from their parents and caretakers according to which violence is valued both positively and negatively, but would integrate into

1. See Urie Bronfenbrenner, *Two Worlds of Childhood* (New York, Russell Sage Foundation, 1970).

their personalities and into their consciousness a value that would reject violence as a mode of human interaction.

Eschewing the use of physical force in rearing children does not mean that inherently nonsocial traits of children would not need to be modified in the course of socialization. It merely means that alternative educational measures would have to replace physical force, since physical force, while perhaps an effective agent of change in human behavior, seems to result in too many undesirable, long-term side effects. Child-rearing literature and practice no doubt offer such alternative means of achieving the socially desirable modifications of nonsocial inclinations of children.

It should be recognized that giving up the use of physical force against children may not be easy for adults who were subjected to physical force and violence in their own childhood and who have adopted the existing value system of American society. Moreover, children can sometimes be very irritating and provocative in their behavior and may strain the tolerance of adults to the limit. Yet in spite of these realities, which must be acknowledged and faced openly, society needs to work toward the gradual reduction and, eventually, complete elimination of physical violence toward its young generation if it is serious about its expressed desire to prevent the physical abuse of children.

As a first, concrete step toward developing eventually comprehensive legal sanctions against the use of physical force in rearing children, the Congress of the United States and legislatures of the states could outlaw corporal punishment in schools, juvenile courts, correctional institutions, and other child-care facilities. Such legislation would assure that children would receive the same protection against physical attack outside their homes as the law provides for adult members of society. Moreover, such legislation is also likely to affect child-rearing attitudes and practices in American homes, for it would symbolize society's growing rejection of violence against children.[2]

2. A unique step in the direction recommended here was taken on June 2, 1970, by the United States District Court in Boston when Chief Judge Charles Wyzanski issued a permanent injunction against corporal punishment in any form under any circumstances in all Boston public schools.

To avoid misinterpretations it should be noted here that rejecting corporal punishment does not imply favoring unlimited permissiveness in rearing children. To grow up successfully, children require a sense of security that is inherent in nonarbitrary structures and limits. Understanding adults can establish such structures and limits through love, patience, firmness, consistency, and rational authority. Corporal punishment seems devoid of constructive educational value, since it cannot provide that sense of security and nonarbitrary authority. Rarely, if ever, is corporal punishment administered for the benefit of the attacked child, for usually it serves the immediate needs of the attacking adult who is seeking relief from his uncontrollable anger and stress. And finally, physical attack by an adult on a weak child is not a sign of strength, for it reflects lack of real authority, and surrender to the attacker's own uncontrollable impulses.

2. Poverty, as has been shown, appears to be related to the phenomenon of physical abuse of children in at least four ways. First, the cultural approval of the use of physical force in child-rearing tends to be stronger among the socioeconomically deprived strata of society than among the middle class. Secondly, there seems to be less inhibition to express and discharge aggressive and violent feelings and impulses toward other persons among members of socioeconomically deprived strata than among the middle class. Thirdly, environmental stress and strain are considerably more serious for persons living in poverty than for those enjoying affluence. Finally, the poor have fewer opportunities than the nonpoor for escaping occasionally from child-rearing responsibilities.

These multiple links between poverty and physical abuse of children suggest that one important route toward reducing the incidence and prevalence of child abuse is the elimination of poverty from America's affluent society. No doubt this is only a partial answer to the complex issue of preventing violence against children, but perhaps a very important part of the total answer, and certainly that part without which other preventive efforts may be utterly futile. Eliminating poverty also happens to be that part of the answer for which this nation possesses the necessary resources, assuming willingness to redistribute national wealth more equitably, and for which it possesses the knowledge of how to effect a change — provided that an unambiguous, high priority, national commitment is made to the unconditional elimination of poverty by assuring to all members of society, without discrimination, equal opportunity to the enjoyment of life through:

a. adequate income derived from employment whenever feasible, or assured by means of a system of nonstigmatizing guaranteed-income maintenance based on legal entitlement rather than on charity and bureaucratic discretion;

b. comprehensive health care and social services;

c. decent and adequate housing and neighborhoods, free from the stigmatizing milieu and conditions of many existing public-housing programs;

d. comprehensive education fitting inherent capacities and assuring the realization of each person's potential;

e. cultural and recreational facilities.

3. Deviance and pathology in areas of physical, social, intellectual, and emotional functioning of individuals and of family units were found to be another set of forces that may contribute to the incidence and prevalence of physical abuse of children. Adequate preventive or ameliorative intervention once an individual or a family is affected by such conditions is known to be very complicated. However, it is also known that these conditions tend to be strongly associated with poverty; the elimination of poverty is therefore likely to reduce, though by no means to eliminate, the incidence and prevalence of these various dysfunctional phenomena. The following measures, aimed at the prevention and amelioration of these conditions and at the strengthening of individual and family functioning should be

available in every community as components of a comprehensive program to reduce the incidence of physical abuse of children and also to help individuals and families once abuse has occured:

a. Comprehensive family-planning programs including the repeal of all legislation concerning medical abortions. The availability of family-planning resources and medical abortions are likely to reduce the number of unwanted and rejected children, who are known to be frequently victims of severe physical abuse and even infanticide. Such provisions would assure that no family would have to increase beyond a size desired by parents and beyond their capacity to care for the children. Women, including single women, would not have to become mothers unless they felt ready for this role. It is important to recall in this context that families with many children, and households headed by females, are overrepresented among families involved in physical abuse of children.

b. Family-life education and counseling programs for adolescents and adults in preparation for marriage and after it. Such programs should be developed in accordance with the assumption that there is much to learn about married life and parenthood which one does not know merely on the basis of sexual and chronological maturity, and that marital and parental relationships can be enriched like all human relationships if one is willing to work toward such enrichment. While such programs should be geared primarily to the strengthening of "normal" families, they could also serve as a screening device for the identification of incipient deviance in any area of individual and family functioning. Such programs should be offered within the public school systems of communities in order to avoid their becoming identified in the mind of the public with deviance-focused agencies.

c. A comprehensive, high quality, neighborhood-based, national health service, financed through general tax revenue and geared not only to the treatment of acute and chronic illness, but also to the promotion and assurance of maximum feasible physical and mental health for everyone.

d. A range of high quality, neighborhood-based social, child-welfare, and child-protective services geared to the reduction of environmental and internal stresses on family life, and especially on mothers who carry major responsibility for the child-rearing function. Such stresses are known to precipitate incidents of physical abuse of children, and any measure that would reduce these stresses would also indirectly reduce the incidence of child abuse. Family counseling, homemaker and housekeeping services, mothers' helpers and babysitting services, family and group day-care facilities for preschool and school-age children are all examples of such services. They would all have to be licensed publicly to assure quality. They should be available on a full coverage basis in every community to all groups in the community and not only to the rich or the very poor. Nor should such services be structured as emergency services; they should be for normal situations, in order to prevent emergencies. No mother should be expected to care for her children around the clock, 365 days a year. Substitute care mechanisms should be routinely available to offer mothers opportunities for carefree rest and recreation.

Every community needs also a system of social services geared to the assistance of families and children who cannot live together because of severe relationship and/or reality problems. Physically abused children belong frequently to this category, and in such situations the welfare of the child and of the family may require temporary or permanent separation. The first requirement for dealing adequately with such situations is diagnostic service capable of arriving at sound decisions which take into consideration the circumstances, needs, and rights of all concerned. Next, a community requires access to a variety of facilities for the care of children away from their homes.

The administration of services and provisions suggested here should be based on a constructive and therapeutic rather than a punitive philosophy, if they are to serve the ultimate objective — the reduction of the general level of violence and the raising of the general level of human well being throughout the entire society.

The three sets of measures proposed are aimed at different levels and aspects of physical abuse of children. The first set would attack the culturally determined core of the phenomenon; the second set would attack and eliminate a major condition to which child abuse is linked in many ways; the third set approaches the causes of child abuse indirectly. It would be futile to argue the relative merits of these approaches; all three are important and should be utilized simultaneously. The basic question seems to be not which measure to select for combating child abuse but whether American society is indeed committed to the well being of all its children and to the eradication of all violence toward them, be it violence perpetrated by individual caretakers, or violence perpetrated collectively by society. If the answer to this question is an unambiguous yes, then the means and the knowledge are surely at hand to progress toward this objective.

Appendix A

*Child Abuse Report Forms —
1967 and 1968*

Please use ball point pen.

State of ....

State or County Agency Case Number (optional): ....

CHILD ABUSE REPORT

Instructions: Please complete each item by circling the bold number next to the appropriate category or by supplying the information requested. If more than one child is involved in the same incident, complete a separate report for each child.

1. Name of Abused Child: ....

                                               First   Middle   **Last**

2. Address (prior to incident): ....

                          No.   Street

.... (7-17)

     City or Town   County   State

     Address Unknown **99**

3. Date of Birth:

     Mo. ----- Day ----- Yr. -----   Unknown **99**
        18 19   20 21   22 23

10. Was this injury fatal?

     Yes   **1** (52)
     No   **2**
     Unknown **9**

4. Age (at time of incident):

`___ ___` Yrs. and `___ ___` Mos.   Unknown 99
  24 25   26 27

5. Sex:

Male   1 (28)
Female   2
Unknown   9

6. Race:

White   1 (29)
Non-white   2
Unknown   9

7. Religion:

Roman Catholic   1 (30)
Christian, other than Roman Catholic   2
Jewish   3
Other   4
Unknown   9

8. Date of Child Abuse Incident:

Mo.`___ ___` Day`___ ___` Yr.`___ ___`   Unknown 99
   31 32   33 34   35 36

9. Injuries sustained (Circle all that apply):

None apparent	01 (37)
Bruises, Welts	02 (38)
Sprains, Dislocations	03 (39)
Malnutrition	04 (40)
Freezing	05 (41)
Burns, Scalding	06 (42)
Abrasions, Lacerations	07 (43)
Wounds, Cuts, Punctures	08 (44)
Internal Injuries	09 (45)
Dismemberment	10 (46)
Bone Fracture(s) other than Skull	11 (47)
Skull Fracture	12 (48)
Brain Damage	13 (49)
Other; Specify:	14 (50)
Unknown	99 (51)

11a. Names of Parent(s) and/or Parent Substitute(s) with whom the Abused Child has been living prior to incident:

Mother or Substitute

First ------------ Middle ------------ Last

If name is unknown, circle   8
If no such female in family, circle   0

Father or Substitute

First ------------ Middle ------------ Last

If name is unknown, circle   8
If no such male in family, circle   0

11b. Specific relationship of these persons to Abused Child:

Mother or Substitute

None in family   0 (53)
Natural parent   1
Adoptive parent   2
Step-parent   3
Foster parent   4
Other relative   5
Not related   6
Relationship unknown   9

Father or Substitute

None in family   0 (54)
Natural parent   1
Adoptive parent   2
Step-parent   3
Foster parent   4
Other relative   5
Not related   6
Relationship unknown   9

Please continue to page 2 and remember to reinsert carbon.

151

12. Identity of perpetrator(s):

    Known   **1** (55)   ⎫   If identity of perpetrator(s) is unknown, go directly to question
    Suspected **2**   ⎬   21, skipping questions **13** to **20**. If known or suspected, continue
    Unknown   **9**   ⎭   to next question.

13. Name of suspected
    perpetrator:

                     Unknown **88**   First   Middle   Last

14. Suspected perpetrator's
    address (prior to incident): ‑‑‑‑‑‑‑‑‑‑‑‑‑‑‑‑‑‑‑‑‑‑‑‑‑‑‑‑‑‑‑‑‑‑‑
                             No.   Street

Address Unknown **99**   City or Town   County   State   (56-66)

    If more than 1 perpetrator is involved in the abuse of the child herein reported, please use additional registry form(s) to report on the remaining perpetrator(s). Complete only questions **13** through **20** on the remaining perpetrator(s). Cross out the identification number(s) printed on the additional registry form(s) used and replace them with the identification number printed on this report.

15. Date of Birth: Mo.‑‑‑‑ Day‑‑‑‑ Yr.‑‑‑‑
                     67 68   69 70   71 72
                  Unknown **99**

16. Age (on last birthday):   ‑‑ ‑‑Yrs.   Unknown **99**
                      73 74

17. Sex: Male   **1** (75)
            Female   **2**
            Unknown **9**

23a. Initial source reporting this incident:

    Private Medical Doctor   **1** (11)
    Hospital or Clinic   **2**
    Police   **3**
    Public Social Agency   **4**
    Private Social Agency   **5**
    School or Child Care Facility **6**
    Public Health or Visiting Nurse **7**
    Other   **8**
    Unknown   **9**

23b. Identity of person initially reporting this incident:

    Name:‑‑‑
              First   Middle   Last

18. **Race:** White 1 (76)
   Non-white 2
   Unknown 9

19. **Religion:** Roman Catholic 1 (77)
   Christian, other than
   Roman Catholic 2
   Jewish 3
   Other 4
   Unknown 9

20. **Relationship to Abused Child:** Natural parent 1 (78)
   Adoptive parent 2
   Step-parent 3
   Foster parent 4
   Sibling, half-sibling,
   step-sibling 5
   Other relative 6
   Not related 7
   Unknown 9

21. Have there been prior incidents of child abuse involving:

	Yes	No	Unknown	
Same Child	1	2	9	(2/7)
Other Child(ren) in Same Home	1	2	9	(8)
Same Perpetrator(s)	1	2	9	(9)

22. Was more than one child abused in this incident?
   Yes 1 (10)
   No 2
   Unknown 9

Title: ....

Agency or Organization..(12-13)

Address: .... No. .... Street
   City or Town   County   State

23c. Date incident was initially reported:

Mo.---- ---- Day---- ---- Yr.---- ---- Unknown **99**
   14 15   16 17   18 19

24. Describe on an additional sheet of paper, the circumstances leading up to and surrounding the incident, including immediate dispositions (medical, legal, or welfare). Mark sheet(s) with the identification number printed on this report.

25. Identity of person completing this report:

Name...
   First   Middle   Last

Title:..

Agency or Organization..

Address: .... No. .... Street
   City or Town   County   State (20-30)

26. Date of this Report:

Mo.---- ---- Day---- ---- Yr.---- ----
   31 32   33 34   35 36

Please use ball point pen

State of...

State or County Agency No. (optional):..

CHILD ABUSE REPORT (1968)

Instructions: Please complete each item by circling the **bold** number next to the appropriate category or by supplying the information requested. If more than one child was abused in the same incident, complete a separate report for each child.

1. Name of Abused Child..

First   Middle   Last

2. Address (prior to incident):.. No.

Street   City or Town

County   State

6 7 8 9 10 11 12 13 14 15 16 17 18 19

Address Unknown **99**

3. Age at time of incident:

___ Yrs. ___ Mos.   Unknown **99**
20 21   22 23

10a. Did Abused Child reside in a children's institution at the time of the incident?

Yes   **1** (49)   If **Yes**, skip items
No   **2**   10b. and 10c.
Unknown   **9**

4. Sex:

Male 1 (24)
Female 2
Unknown 9

5. Race:

White 1 (25)
Negro 2
American Indian 3
Puerto Rican 4
Mexican 5
Asian 6
Other; Specify: ----- 7
Unknown 9

6. Religion:

Roman Catholic 1 (26)
Christian, other than R.C. 2
Jewish 3
Muslim 4
Other; Specify: ----- 5
Unknown 9

7. Date of Child Abuse Incident:

Mo. ___ Day ___ Yr ___ Unknown 99
   27 28   29 30

8. Injuries sustained (Circle all that apply):

None apparent	31
Bruises, Welts	32
Abrasions, Lacerations	33
Wounds, Cuts, Punctures	34
Sprains, Dislocations	35
Internal Injuries	36
Bone Fracture(s) other than Skull	37
Dismemberment	38
Exposure, Freezing	39
Burns, Scalding	40
Skull Fracture	41
Subdural Hemorrhage or Hematoma	42
Brain Damage	43
Poisoning	44
Malnutrition (due to deliberate withholding of food)	45
Other; Specify: -----	46
Unknown	47

9. Was the injury fatal?

Yes 1 (48)
No 2
Unknown 9

10b. Names of Parent(s) and/or Parent Substitute(s) with whom the Abused Child has been living prior to this incident:

Mother or Substitute:

First	Middle	Last
Mother's or Substitute's name unknown		0 (50)
Not known whether mother or substitute in family		7
No mother or substitute in family		8

Father or Substitute:

First	Middle	Last
Father's or Substitute's name unknown		0 (51)
Not known whether father or substitute in family		7
No father or substitute in family		8

10c. Relationship to Abused Child of Parent(s) and/or Parent Substitute(s):

	Mother or Substitute	Father or Substitute
None in family	8 (50)	8 (51)
Natural parent	1	1
Adoptive parent	2	2
Step-parent (legal or non-legal)	3	3
Foster parent	4	4
Other relative	5	5
Not related	6	6
Relationship unknown	9	9

11. Have there been prior incidents of Child Abuse involving:

	Same child	Other children in same family
Yes	1 (52)	1 (53)
No	2	2
Unknown	9	9

155

Information on (suspected) perpetrator

If more than 1 perpetrator is involved in the abuse of the child herein reported, use additional report form(s) to report on the remaining perpetrator(s). Complete only questions 18 through 26 on the remaining perpetrator form(s). Replace the identification number(s) of the additional report form(s) with the identification number printed on this report.

12. Has a Child Abuse report been filed on this child during 1968 prior to this report?

Yes   1 (54)
No   2
Unknown   9

13. Number of children abused in the current incident: ___ ___ 55 56

Unknown   99

14. Initial medical or official resource dealing with this incident:

Private Medical Doctor   1 (57)
Hospital or Clinic   2
Police   3
Public Social Agency   4
Private Social Agency   5
School or Child Care Facility   6
Public Health or Visiting Nurse   7
Other; Specify   8
Unknown   9

15. Person initially reporting this incident:

Name: First   Middle   Last

Title:

Agency or Organization:

Address: No.   Street

City or Town   County   State

16. Date incident was reported initially on local level:

Mo.___ 58 59   Day ___ 60 61   Yr.____   Unknown   99

19. Name of (suspected) perpetrator:

63 64 65 66 67 68

First   Middle   Last   Unknown   99

20. Address: (prior to incident)

No.   Street

City or Town   County   State

Address Unknown   99

21. Age: (on last birthday) ___ ___ 69 70   Unknown   99

22. Sex:

Male   1 (71)
Female   2
Unknown   9

23. Race:

White   1 (72)
Negro   2
American Indian   3
Puerto Rican   4
Mexican   5
Asian   6
Other; Specify   7
Unknown   9

24. Religion:

Roman Catholic   1 (73)
Christian, other than R.C.   2
Jewish   3
Muslim   4
Other; Specify   5
Unknown   9

17. Describe on an additional sheet of paper, the circumstances leading up to and surrounding the incident, including immediate dispositions (medical, legal, or welfare). Mark sheet(s) with the identification number printed on this report.

18. Identity of perpetrator(s):

Known   **1** (62)
Suspected   **2**
Unknown   **9**

If identity of perpetrator(s) is unknown skip questions 19 through 26. If known or suspected, continue to next question.

Person completing this report:

Name: --

Title: ---

Agency or Organization: --------------------------------

Address: -------------------------   -------------------------
         No.   Street

-------------------------   -------------------------   -------------------------
City or Town   County   State

Date of this report:

Mo.____ — Day____ — Yr.____ —

25. Specific relationship to Abused Child of (suspected) perpetrator:

Natural parent ----------------------------------- **1** (74)
Adoptive parent --------------------------------- **2**
Step-parent (legal or non-legal) -------------- **3**
Foster parent ------------------------------------ **4**
Other relative; Specify: ----------------------- **5**
Teacher or school personnel ------------------- **6**
Personnel in child-care facility ---------------- **7**
Other; Specify: --------------------------------- **8**

Unknown --------------------------------------- **9**

26. Have there been prior incidents of Child Abuse involving the same perpetrator?

Yes   **1** (75)
No   **2**
Unknown   **9**

27. Follow-up classification

Abuse confirmed   **1** (76)
Abuse ruled out   **2**
Uncertain   **3**
No follow-up as yet   **9**

Nationwide Study of Child Abuse
conducted by
Brandeis University, Waltham, Mass.
For
Children's Bureau
U. S. Department of Health, Education and Welfare

157

Appendix B

Sample Design and Sampling Units

NATIONWIDE EPIDEMIOLOGIC STUDY OF CHILD ABUSE
Sampling Design and Units

	REGIONS		
Definition of strata and substrata	I. W & SW (17 states)	II. MW & NE (17 states)	III. MA & S (16 states)
1. 10 largest SMSAs 2,000,000+			
1a. core cities	Los Angeles, Cal. San Francisco, Cal. St. Louis, Mo.	Chicago, Ill. Detroit, Mich. Boston, Mass.	New York, New York Pittsburgh, Pa. (Philadelphia, Pa.) (Washington, D.C.)
1b. non-core components 500,000+	St. Louis County, Mo.	Cook County, Ill.	Westchester County, N.Y.
1c. non-core components under 500,000	San Mateo County, Cal.	DuPage County, Ill.	Prince George's County, Md.
2. SMSAs under 2,000,000 with core cities 250,000+			
2a. core cities 400,000+	Seattle, Wash.	Columbus, Ohio	Baltimore, Md.
2b. core cities 250,000 to under 400,000	Oklahoma City, Oklahoma	Dayton, Ohio	Louisville, Kentucky
2c. non-core components 100,000+	Multnomah County, Ore. (excl. Portland)	Summit County, Ohio (excl. Akron)	Baltimore County, Md.
2d. non-core components under 100,000	Osage County, Oklahoma (excl. Tulsa)	Clermont County, Ohio	Wayne County, N.Y.
3. SMSAs under 2,000,000 with core cities under 250,000			
3a. core cities 100,000 to under 250,000	Lubbock, Texas	Madison, Wis.	Nashville, Tenn.
3b. core cities under 100,000	Boise City, Idaho	Fargo, N.D.	Macon, Georgia
3c. non-core components 100,000+	Maricopa County, Arizona (excl. Phoenix)	Worcester County (part), Mass. (excl. Worcester)	Palm Beach, Fla. (excl. West Palm Beach)
3d. non-core components under 100,000	Taylor County, Texas (excl. Abilene)	Middlesex County (part), Conn.	Fayette County, Ky. (excl. Lexington)
Total No. Units within SMSAs	13	13	12 (+ 2)

Appendix C

Research Schedule — Abused Child

Agency Case No. (Optional): _____

NATIONWIDE EPIDEMIOLOGIC STUDY OF CHILD ABUSE

CHILDREN'S BUREAU

WELFARE ADMINISTRATION

U. S. DEPARTMENT OF HEALTH, EDUCATION, AND WELFARE

Conducted by:

THE FLORENCE HELLER GRADUATE SCHOOL FOR ADVANCED STUDIES IN SOCIAL WELFARE

BRANDEIS UNIVERSITY

WALTHAM, MASSACHUSETTS

Schedule A: Abused Child

Instructions: Complete a separate schedule on each abused child whose abuse has either been established beyond doubt or by virtue of circumstantial evidence by circling the number next to the appropriate category or by supplying the information requested.

1. NAME OF
   ABUSED CHILD: _____
                     First   *Middle*   *Last*

2. CASE STATUS:

Abuse established beyond doubt	1	(6)
Strong circumstantial evidence of abuse	2	
Weak circumstantial evidence of abuse	3	

3. BIRTHDATE AND AGE:

Birthdate: Mo. __ __ Day __ __ Yr. __ __
　　　　　　 7　8　　　　9　10　　　11　12

　　　Unknown　99

Age (at time of incident): __ __ Yrs. and __ __ Mos.
　　　　　　　　　　　　　 13　14　　　　　 15　16

　　　Unknown　99

4. SEX:

Male	1	(17)
Female	2	
Unknown	9	

5. ETHNIC BACKGROUND:

White	1	(18)
Negro	2	
American Indian	3	
Puerto Rican	4	
Mexican	5	
Asian	6	
Other; specify:	7	
Unknown	9	

6. RELIGIOUS BACKGROUND:

Roman Catholic	1	(19)
Christian, other than Roman Catholic	2	
Jewish	3	
Other; specify:	4	
Unknown	9	

7. SCHOOL AND EMPLOYMENT STATUS PRIOR TO INCIDENT:

Under school age	01	(20-21)
Of school age, never attended school	02	
Grade appropriate for age	03	
Grade below age level, or in class for retarded	04	
Advanced grade placement	05	
Did not complete high school, unemployed	06	
Did not complete high school, employed	07	
Completed high school, unemployed	08	
Completed high school, employed	09	
Completed high school, entered college	10	
Other; specify:	11	
Unknown	99	

8. REGULAR WHEREABOUTS OF NATURAL (BIOLOGICAL) PARENTS PRIOR TO INCIDENT:

	Mother		Father	
In child's home	1	(22)	1	(23)
Not in home, whereabouts known	2		2	
Not in home, whereabouts unknown	3		3	
Deceased	4		4	
Unknown	9		9	

9. NOTICEABLE DEVIATIONS OF ABUSED CHILD FROM THE FOLLOWING AREAS OF NORMAL FUNCTIONING DURING 12 MONTHS PRIOR TO INCIDENT (*CIRCLE ALL THAT APPLY*):

Physical	1	(24-26)
Intellectual	2	
Social or Behavioral	3	

10. HAD THE CHILD HAD ANY OF THE FOLLOWING EXPERIENCES PRIOR TO INCIDENT? (*CIRCLE ALL THAT APPLY*):

Hospitalization for physical illness	1	(27-32)
Hospitalization for mental illness	2	
Juvenile court (except traffic)	3	
Foster family care	4	
Child care institution	5	
Correctional institution	6	

11. HAD CHILD BEEN INVOLVED IN INCIDENTS OF
    ABUSE PRIOR TO THIS INCIDENT?

	Yes	No	Unknown	
As victim	1	2	9	(33)
As perpetrator	1	2	9	(34)

12. DATE ON WHICH CURRENT INCIDENT OCCURRED:

    Mo. __ __ Day __ __ Yr. __ __
       35 36   37 38   39 40

    Unknown 99

13. APPROXIMATE TIME AT WHICH CURRENT INCIDENT
    OCCURRED:

12:01 - 3 AM	1	(41)
3:01 - 6 AM	2	
6:01 - 9 AM	3	
9:01 - 12 Noon	4	
12:01 - 3 PM	5	
3:01 - 6 PM	6	
6:01 - 9 PM	7	
9:01 - 12 Midnight	8	
Unknown	9	

14. PLACE WHERE CURRENT INCIDENT OCCURRED:

Child's household	1	(42)
Perpetrator's household (if not a regular member in child's household)	2	
School	3	
Child-care facility	4	
Public place	5	
Other; specify:	6	
Unkown	9	

15. PERSONS [OTHER THAN SUSPECTED PERPETRATOR(S)] PRESENT AT SCENE WHEN CURRENT INCIDENT OCCURRED (*CIRCLE ALL THAT APPLY*):

Mother or Mother Substitute	1	(43-50)
Father or Father Substitute	2	
Other regular member(s) of household 18 years of age or older	3	
Other regular member(s) of household under 18 years of age	4	
Relative(s) outside household 18 or older	5	
Relative(s) outside household under 18	6	
Non-related person(s) outside household 18 or older	7	
Non-related person(s) outside household under 18	8	

16. TYPES OF INJURIES SUSTAINED IN PRESENT INCIDENT (*CIRCLE ALL THAT APPLY*):

None	01	(51-66)
Bruises, Welts	02	
Sprains, Dislocations	03	
Malnutrition	04	
Freezing	05	
Burns, Scalding	06	
Abrasions, Contusions, Lacerations	07	
Wounds, Cuts, Punctures	08	
Internal Injuries	09	
Dismemberment	10	
Bone Fracture(s) other than Skull	11	
Skull Fracture	12	
Subdural Hemorrhage or Hematoma	13	
Brain Damage	14	
Other; specify:	15	
Unknown	99	

17. HAVE THESE INJURIES BEEN VERIFIED MEDICALLY?

Yes	1	(67)
No	2	
Unknown	9	

18. MANNER BY WHICH THESE INJURIES WERE
    INFLICTED (*CIRCLE ALL THAT APPLY*):

Beating with hands	01	(4/6-18)
Beating with instruments	02	
Kicking	03	
Strangling or Suffocating	04	
Drowning	05	
Shooting	06	
Stabbing or Slashing	07	
Burning or Scalding	08	
Poisoning	09	
Deliberate neglect or exposure	10	
Locking in or Tying	11	
Other; specify:	12	
Unknown	99	

19. SERIOUSNESS OF THESE INJURIES:

Not serious	1	(19)
Serious, no permanent damage expected	2	
Serious, permanent damage expected	3	
Fatal	4	
Unknown	9	

20. HAS THE DEGREE OF SERIOUSNESS BEEN
    VERIFIED MEDICALLY?

Yes	1	(20)
No	2	
Unknown	9	

21. WHO INITIATED HELP FOR THE CHILD
    SUBSEQUENT TO CURRENT INCIDENT?
    (*CIRCLE ALL THAT APPLY*):

Suspected perpetrator(s)	1	(21-24)
Member(s) of child's household [excluding perpetrator(s)]	2	
School or child-care personnel [excluding perpetrator(s)]	3	
Other [excluding perpetrator(s)]; specify:	4	

22. RESOURCE *FIRST* CONTACTED FOR MEDICAL OR OFFI-
CIAL ASSISTANCE SUBSEQUENT TO CURRENT INCIDENT:

Private Medical Doctor	1	(25)
Hospital or Clinic	2	
Police	3	
Public Social Agency	4	
Private Social Agency	5	
Other; specify:	6	
Unknown	9	

23. TIME BETWEEN INCIDENT AND THIS INITIAL CONTACT
SUBSEQUENT TO CURRENT INCIDENT:

Less than 3 hours	1	(26)
3 to under 12 hours	2	
12 to under 24 hours	3	
1 day to under 2 days	4	
2 days to under 1 week	5	
1 week to under 1 month	6	
1 month or more	7	
Unknown	9	

24. MEDICAL TREATMENT RENDERED TO CHILD
SUBSEQUENT TO CURRENT INCIDENT:

No medical treatment	1	(27)
Hospitalization 1 day or under	2	
Hospitalization 2 to 7 days	3	
Hospitalization 8 to 30 days	4	
Hospitalization over 30 days	5	
Other medical treatment, one visit only	6	
Other medical treatment, more than one visit	7	
Other; specify:	8	
Unknown	9	

25a. AGENCY INVOLVEMENT IN CASE SUBSEQUENT TO
CURRENT INCIDENT (*CIRCLE ALL THAT APPLY*):

Police	1	(28-31)
District or County Attorney	2	
Court	3	
Social Agency	4	

25b. AGENCY DISPOSITION AND ACTIVITIES IN CASE
SUBSEQUENT TO CURRENT INCIDENT (*CIRCLE
ALL THAT APPLY*):

Services in office or client's home (excluding homemaker service)	1	(32-39)
Homemaker service	2	
Placement of Abused Child	3	
Placement of other children	4	
Suspected perpetrator(s) indicted	5	
Indicted perpetrator(s) convicted	6	
Convicted perpetrator(s) jailed	7	
Other; specify:	8	

26. PLEASE DESCRIBE IN DETAIL THE CIRCUMSTANCES
LEADING UP TO AND SURROUNDING CURRENT INCIDENT:

_____

_____

_____

_____

_____

_____

_____

_____

_____

_____

_____

(continue to next page)

(continue to next page)

27. SPECIFIC RELATIONSHIP TO ABUSED CHILD OF PARENT(S) AND/OR PARENT SUBSTITUTE(S) WITH WHOM THIS CHILD HAS BEEN REGULARLY LIVING PRIOR TO INCIDENT:

Mother or Substitute		*Father or Substitute*	
None living in family	0 (40)	None living in family	0 (41)
Natural parent	1	Natural parent	1
Adoptive parent	2	Adoptive parent	2
Stepparent (legal or non-legal)	3	Stepparent (legal or non-legal)	3
Foster parent	4	Foster parent	4
Other relative	6	Other relative	6
Not related	7	Not related	7
Relationship unknown	9	Relationship unknown	9

28. HAVE OTHER CHILDREN IN THE FAMILY (OTHER THAN CHILD DESCRIBED IN THIS SCHEDULE) *PREVIOUSLY* BEEN INVOLVED IN INCIDENTS OF ABUSE?

	Yes	*No*	*Unknown*
As victim	1	2	9 (42)
As perpetrator	1	2	9 (43)

29. HAVE OTHER CHILDREN IN THE FAMILY (OTHER THAN CHILD DESCRIBED IN THIS SCHEDULE) BEEN ABUSED IN THE *CURRENT* INCIDENT?

Yes	1	(44)
No	2	
Unknown	9	

If "Yes" ("1" above), the following Questions 30 through 51 should be completed on the schedule of ONE child in the family only. On the schedules of the remaining abused children, simply write in the space provided below the identification number of the ONE child for whom Questions 30 through 51 have been answered and skip to Question 52.

Identification Number: __ __ __ __ __
45 46 47 48 49

Please be sure to answer Questions 52 through 55 on the schedules "A" (white) of ALL abused children.

175

30. BIRTHDATE AND AGE OF PARENT(S) AND/OR PARENT SUBSTITUTE(S):

MOTHER OR SUBSTITUTE
If no such female living in family, circle   00

Birthdate: Mo. __ __ Day __ __ Yr. __ __   If unknown, circle   99
                     50 51   52 53   54 55

Age (at last birthdate): __ __ Yrs. If unknown, circle   99
                                      56 57

FATHER OR SUBSTITUTE
If no such male living in family, circle   00

Birthdate: Mo. __ __ Day __ __ Yr. __ __   If unknown, circle   99
                     58 59   60 61   62 63

Age (at last birthdate): __ __ Yrs. If unknown, circle   99
                                      64 65

31. ETHNIC BACKGROUND OF PARENT(S) AND/OR PARENT SUBSTITUTE(S):

	Mother or Substitute	*Father or Substitute*
None living in family	0 (66)	0 (67)
White	1	1
Negro	2	2
American Indian	3	3
Puerto Rican	4	4
Mexican	5	5
Asian	6	6
Other; specify:	7	7
Unknown	9	9

32. RELIGIOUS BACKGROUND OF PARENT(S) AND/OR SUBSTITUTE(S):

	Mother or Substitute	*Father or Substitute*
None living in family	0 (68)	0 (69)
Roman Catholic	1	1
Christian, other than Roman Catholic	2	2
Jewish	3	3
Other; specify:	4	4
Unknown	9	9

33. MARITAL STATUS OF PARENT(S) AND/OR PARENT
    SUBSTITUTE(S) PRIOR TO INCIDENT:

	Mother or Substitute	Father or Substitute
None living in family	0 (70)	0 (71)
Single, never married	1	1
Separated, Divorced, Deserted, or Widowed	2	2
Living with spouse (legal or non-legal)	3	3
Unknown	9	9

34. HIGHEST LEVEL OF EDUCATION COMPLETED BY
    PARENT(S) AND/OR SUBSTITUTE(S) PRIOR TO INCIDENT:

	Mother or Substitute	Father or Substitute
None living in family	0 (72)	0 (73)
Never attended school	1	1
Less than 9 grades	2	2
9 to under 12 grades	3	3
High school graduate	4	4
Some college or technical school	5	5
College graduate	6	6
Master's degree	7	7
Doctoral degree	8	8
Unknown	9	9

35. EMPLOYMENT STATUS PRIOR TO INCIDENT:

	Mother or Substitute	Father or Substitute
None living in family	0 (74)	0 (75)
Retired	1	1
Permanently disabled	2	2
Temporarily disabled	3	3
Unemployed, but available for work	4	4
Employed part time (under 35 hours per week)	5	5
Employed full time (35 hours per week or over)	6	6
Housekeeping only (own home)	7	7
Unknown	9	9

36. CUSTOMARY OCCUPATION, INCLUDING SELF-EMPLOYMENT:

MOTHER OR SUBSTITUTE

Specify and describe in detail: _____

_____

_____

_____ (5/6-9)

If no such female living in family, circle   00   If unknown, circle   99

FATHER OR SUBSTITUTE

Specify and describe in detail: _____

_____

_____

_____ (10-13)

If no such male living in family, circle   00   If unknown, circle   99

37. CIRCLE THAT CATEGORY ON THE BUREAU OF CENSUS OCCUPATIONAL RATING CODE WHICH MOST NEARLY APPLIES:

	Mother or Substitute	Father or Substitute
None living in family	00 (14-15)	00 (16-17)
Professional, technical, Professional, technical or kindred worker	01	01
Farm or farm manager	02	02
Manager, official, proprietor, excluding farm	03	03
Clerical or kindred worker	04	04
Sales worker	05	05
Craftsman, foreman, or kindred worker	06	06
Operative or kindred worker	07	07
Private household worker	08	08
Service worker, excluding private household	09	09
Farm laborer or foreman	10	10
Laborer, excluding farm	11	11
Housekeeping only (own home)	12	12
Unknown	99	99

38. TOTAL DURATION OF FULL OR PART-TIME GAINFUL EMPLOYMENT (INCLUDING SELF-EMPLOYMENT) OF PARENT(S) AND/OR SUBSTITUTE(S) DURING 12 MONTHS PRIOR TO INCIDENT:

	Mother or Substitute	Father or Substitute
None living in family	0 (18)	0 (19)
Employed entire 12 months	1	1
9 to under 12 months	2	2
6 to under 9 months	3	3
3 to under 6 months	4	4
Less than 3 months	5	5
Unemployed entire 12 months	6	6
Housekeeping only (own home)	7	7
Unknown	9	9

39. NOTICEABLE DEVIATIONS OF PARENT(S) AND/OR SUBSTITUTE(S) FROM FOLLOWING AREAS OF NORMAL FUNCTIONING DURING 12 MONTHS PRIOR TO INCIDENT (*CIRCLE ALL THAT APPLY*):

Mother or Substitute
- Physical   1 (20-22)
- Intellectual   2
- Social or Behavioral   3

If no such female living in family, circle   0

Father or Substitute
- Physical   1 (23-25)
- Intellectual   2
- Social or Behavioral   3

If no such male living in family, circle   0

40. HAD PARENT(S) AND/OR SUBSTITUTE(S) HAD ANY OF THE FOLLOWING EXPERIENCES PRIOR TO INCIDENT? (*CIRCLE ALL THAT APPLY*):

Mother or Substitute

Hospitalization for mental illness	1	(26-29)
Juvenile court (except traffic) as youngster	2	
Placement away from home as youngster	3	
Criminal conviction	4	

If no such female living in family, circle   0

Father or Substitute

Hospitalization for mental illness	1	(30-33)
Juvenile court (except traffic) as youngster	2	
Placement away from home as youngster	3	
Criminal conviction	4	

If no such male living in family, circle   0

41. HAVE PARENT(S) AND/OR SUBSTITUTE(S) BEEN INVOLVED IN INCIDENTS OF ABUSE PRIOR TO INCIDENT?

Mother or Substitute		*Yes*	*No*	*Unknown*	
	As victim	1	2	9	(34)
	As perpetrator	1	2	9	(35)

If no such female living in family, circle   0

Father or Substitute		*Yes*	*No*	*Unknown*	
	As victim	1	2	9	(36)
	As perpetrator	1	2	9	(37)

If no such male living in family, circle   0

42. TOTAL NUMBER OF PERSONS UNDER 18 YEARS OF AGE
REGULARLY LIVING IN FAMILY PRIOR TO INCIDENT:

    Specify number of persons: __ __
                              38 39

        Unknown   99

43. TOTAL NUMBER OF PERSONS 18 YEARS OF AGE OR
OLDER REGULARLY LIVING IN FAMILY PRIOR TO INCIDENT:

    Specify number of persons: __ __
                              40 41

        Unknown   99

44. GROSS MONTHLY INCOME IN ABUSED CHILD'S FAMILY
DURING MONTH PRIOR TO INCIDENT:

    Specify approximate dollar amount: __ __ __ __
                                     42 43 44 45

        Unknown   9999

45. SOURCES OF THIS INCOME (*CIRCLE ALL THAT APPLY*):

Employment of family members	1	(46-53)
Other members of household	2	
Relatives outside household	3	
AFDC	4	
Other public assistance	5	
Social Security	6	
Unemployment compensation	7	
Other; specify:	8	

46. SERVICES AND/OR FINANCIAL ASSISTANCE RECEIVED
BY ANY MEMBERS OF ABUSED CHILD'S FAMILY FROM
PUBLIC OR VOLUNTARY SOCIAL WELFARE AGENCIES
PRIOR TO INCIDENT:

	Public		Voluntary	
None	0	(54)	0	(55)
Received before 1/1/67 only	1		1	
Received before and after 1/1/67	2		2	
Received after 1/1/67 only	3		3	
Unknown	9		9	

47. **TYPE OF HOUSING ACCOMMODATIONS OF ABUSED CHILD'S FAMILY PRIOR TO INCIDENT:**

Rented apartment in public housing	1	(56)
Rented house in public housing	2	
Rented apartment in private building	3	
Rented house from private owner	4	
Privately owned apartment in cooperative	5	
Privately owned home	6	
Trailer (owned or rented)	7	
Other; specify:	8	
Unknown	9	

48. **NUMBER OF ROOMS IN LIVING QUARTERS OF ABUSED CHILD'S FAMILY PRIOR TO INCIDENT:**

Specify number of rooms: __ __
57 58

Unknown 99

49. **COST OF HOUSING (INCLUDING UTILITIES) FOR MONTH PRIOR TO INCIDENT:**

Specify approximate dollar amount: __ __ __
59 60 61

Unknown 999

50. **LENGTH OF TIME IN THESE ACCOMMODATIONS PRIOR TO INCIDENT:**

Less than one year	00

Specify approximate number of years: __ __
62 63

Unknown 99

51. DID CHILD'S FAMILY REGULARLY SHARE LIVING QUARTERS WITH OTHERS PRIOR TO INCIDENT:

Yes	1	(64)
No	2	
Unknown	9	

52. IDENTITY OF PERPETRATOR(S) IN CURRENT INCIDENT:

Neither known nor suspected	1	(65)
Suspected	2	
Established by court procedures	3	
Established by other than court procedures	4	

If "neither known nor suspected" ("1" above), go directly to Question 55, skipping Questions 53 and 54. Otherwise, continue to next question.

53. RELATIONSHIP OF PERPETRATOR(S) TO ABUSED CHILD:

	Perpetrator #1		Perpetrator #2		Perpetrator #3	
Mother or Substitute living with child	1	(66)	1	(67)	1	(68)
Father or Substitute living with child	2		2		2	
Other	3		3		3	
Relationship Unknown	9		9		9	

If more than three perpetrators are involved, add another sheet and list each additional perpetrator, indicating his relationship to the abused child according to the foregoing categories. Identify the additional sheet by marking it with the identification number printed on this schedule.

Please complete a separate schedule "B" (pink) on each perpetrator who is not a parent or parent substitute with whom the abused child has been living prior to incident. In other words, complete a separate schedule on those perpetrator(s) not checked as parent(s) and/or parent substitute(s) in Question 53 above.

54. IN PLACES PROVIDED BELOW, WRITE THE IDENTIFI-
CATION NUMBERS PRINTED ON THE SCHEDULES "B"
(PINK) WHICH YOU WILL HAVE COMPLETED ON
EACH PERPETRATOR:

Perpetrator Identification number: __ __ __ __ __
6/6 7   8   9   10

Perpetrator Identification number: __ __ __ __ __
11 12 13 14 15

Perpetrator Identification number: __ __ __ __ __
16 17 18 19 20

Perpetrator Identification number: __ __ __ __ __
21 22 23 24 25

55. IN CASE WE WISH TO SEEK ADDITIONAL INFORMATION,
PLEASE SUPPLY:

Date (Schedule completed):_____

Mo. Day Yr.

Your name:_____
First   Middle   Last

Title:_____

Agency name:_____

Address:_____
No.   Street

_____
City or Town   County   State (26-36)

Telephone and extension number:_____

THANK YOU FOR YOUR PARTICIPATION IN THIS STUDY.
WE WILL SEND TO YOU A COPY OF OUR FINAL REPORT.

Appendix D

Research Schedule — Perpetrator

NATIONWIDE EPIDEMIOLOGIC STUDY OF CHILD ABUSE

CHILDREN'S BUREAU

WELFARE ADMINISTRATION

U.S. DEPARTMENT OF HEALTH, EDUCATION, AND WELFARE

Conducted by:

THE FLORENCE HELLER GRADUATE SCHOOL FOR ADVANCED STUDIES IN SOCIAL WELFARE

BRANDEIS UNIVERSITY
WALTHAM, MASSACHUSETTS

Schedule B: Suspected Perpetrator

Instructions: Complete a separate schedule on each suspected perpetrator by circling the number next to the appropriate category or by supplying the information requested. [If perpetrator(s) are parent(s) and/or parent substitute(s) with whom the abused child has been living prior to the incident, *do not* complete a separate schedule "B."]

1. NAME OF SUSPECTED
   PERPETRATOR: _____

                                   First   *Middle*   *Last*

2. RELATIONSHIP OF SUSPECTED PERPETRATOR TO ABUSED CHILD:

Natural (biological) parent *not* living in household
of Abused Child   1 (6)

Adoptive parent *not* living in household of
Abused Child   2

Stepparent *not* living in household of Abused Child   3

Sibling, Half sibling, or Stepsibling   5

Other relative; specify: 6

Not related   7

Relationship unknown   9

3. BIRTHDATE AND AGE OF SUSPECTED PERPETRATOR:

Birthdate: Mo. __ __ Day __ __ Yr. __ __
          7 8   9 10   11 12

Unknown 99

Age (at last birthdate): __ __ Yrs.
          13 14

Unknown 99

4. SEX:

Female   1 (15)

Male   2

Unknown   9

5. ETHNIC BACKGROUND:

White   1 (16)

Negro   2

American Indian   3

Puerto Rican   4

Mexican   5

Asian   6

Other; specify: 7

Unknown   9

6. RELIGIOUS BACKGROUND:

    Roman Catholic   1 (17)

    Christian, other than Roman Catholic 2

    Jewish   3

    Other; specify: 4

    Unknown   9

7. MARITAL STATUS PRIOR TO INCIDENT:

    Living without spouse (legal or non-legal)
        but with children   2 (18)

    Living with spouse (legal or non-legal)
        and with children   3

    Living without spouse (legal or non-legal)
        and without children   4

    Living with spouse (legal or non-legal)
        but without children   5

    Unknown   9

8. HAD SUSPECTED PERPETRATOR BEEN A PARENT OR PARENT SUBSTITUTE PRIOR TO INCIDENT?

    Yes   1 (19)

    No   2

    Unknown   9

9. HIGHEST LEVEL OF EDUCATION COMPLETED PRIOR TO INCIDENT:

    Never attended school   1 (20)

    Less than 9 grades   2

    9 to under 12 grades   3

    High school graduate   4

    Some college or technical school   5

    College graduate   6

    Master's degree   7

    Doctoral degree   8

    Unknown   9

10. EMPLOYMENT STATUS PRIOR TO INCIDENT:

Student	0 (21)
Retired	1
Permanently disabled	2
Temporarily disabled	3
Unemployed, but available for work	4
Employed part time (under 35 hours per week)	5
Employed full time (35 hours per week or over)	6
Housekeeping only (own home)	7
Unknown	9

11a. CUSTOMARY OCCUPATION (INCLUDING SELF-EMPLOYMENT):

Specify and describe in detail: _____

_____

_____

_____(22-25)

       If unknown, circle   99

11b. CIRCLE THAT CATEGORY ON THE BUREAU OF CENSUS OCCUPATIONAL RATING CODE WHICH MOST NEARLY APPLIES:

Professional, technical, or kindred worker	01 (26-27)
Farm or farm manager	02
Manager, official, proprietor, excluding farm	03
Clerical or kindred worker	04
Sales worker	05
Craftsman, foreman, or kindred worker	06
Operative or kindred worker	07
Private household worker	08
Service worker, excluding private household	09
Farm laborer or foreman	10
Laborer, excluding farm	11
Housekeeping only (own home)	12
Unknown	99

12. TOTAL DURATION OF FULL OR PART-TIME GAINFUL
EMPLOYMENT (INCLUDING SELF-EMPLOYMENT) DURING
12 MONTHS PRIOR TO INCIDENT:

Employed entire 12 months	1	(28)
9 to under 12 months	2	
6 to under 9 months	3	
3 to under 6 months	4	
Less than 3 months	5	
Unemployed entire 12 months	6	
Housekeeping only (own home)	7	
Unknown	9	

13. NOTICEABLE DEVIATIONS FROM FOLLOWING AREAS OF
NORMAL FUNCTIONING DURING 12 MONTHS PRIOR TO
INCIDENT (*CIRCLE ALL THAT APPLY*):

Physical	1	(29-31)
Intellectual	2	
Social or Behavioral	3	

14. HAD SUSPECTED PERPETRATOR HAD ANY OF THE
FOLLOWING EXPERIENCES PRIOR TO INCIDENT?
(*CIRCLE ALL THAT APPLY*):

Hospitalization for mental illness	1	(32-35)
Juvenile court (except traffic) as youngster	2	
Placement away from home as youngster	3	
Criminal conviction	4	

15. HAD SUSPECTED PERPETRATOR BEEN INVOLVED IN
INCIDENTS OF ABUSE PRIOR TO THIS INCIDENT?

	Yes	No	Unknown	
As victim	1	2	9	(36)
As perpetrator	1	2	9	(37)

16. IS SUSPECTED PERPETRATOR A REGULAR MEMBER IN
THE FAMILY OF ANY CHILD ABUSED IN THE CURRENT
INCIDENT?

Yes	1	(38)
No	2	
Unknown	9	

If "yes" ("1" above), copy the identification number from child's schedule
"A" here __ __ __ __ __, and go directly to Question 28, skipping Questions
   39 40 41 42 43
17 through 27. If "no" ("2" above), complete all remaining Questions (17
through 28) on this schedule.

17. TOTAL NUMBER OF PERSONS UNDER 18 YEARS OF AGE
REGULARLY LIVING IN PERPETRATOR'S FAMILY
PRIOR TO INCIDENT:

   Specify number of persons: __ __
                            44 45

      Unknown 99

18. TOTAL NUMBER OF PERSONS 18 YEARS OF AGE
OR OLDER REGULARLY LIVING IN PERPETRATOR'S
FAMILY PRIOR TO INCIDENT:

   Specify number of persons: __ __
                            46 47

      Unknown 99

19. HAD ANY PERSON(S) IN PERPETRATOR'S FAMILY (OTHER
THAN SUSPECTED PERPETRATOR) EVER BEEN INVOLVED
IN INCIDENTS OF ABUSE PRIOR TO THIS INCIDENT?

	Yes	No	Unknown	
As victim	1	2	9	(48)
As perpetrator	1	2	9	(49)

   If no other persons living in family, circle 0

20. GROSS MONTHLY INCOME IN SUSPECTED PERPETRATOR'S
FAMILY DURING MONTH PRIOR TO INCIDENT:

   Specify approximate dollar amount: __ __ __ __
                                  50 51 52 53

      Unknown 9999

21. SOURCES OF THIS INCOME (CIRCLE ALL THAT APPLY):

Employment of family members	1	(54-61)
Other members of household	2	
Relatives outside household	3	
AFDC	4	
Other public assistance	5	
Social Security	6	
Unemployment compensation	7	
Other; specify:	8	

22. SERVICES AND/OR FINANCIAL ASSISTANCE RECEIVED BY ANY MEMBER(S) OF SUSPECTED PERPETRATOR'S FAMILY FROM PUBLIC OR VOLUNTARY SOCIAL WELFARE AGENCIES PRIOR TO INCIDENT:

	Public	Voluntary
None	0 (62)	0 (63)
Received before 1/1/67 only	1	1
Received before and after 1/1/67	2	2
Received after 1/1/67 only	3	3
Unknown	9	9

23. TYPE OF HOUSING ACCOMMODATIONS OF SUSPECTED PERPETRATOR'S FAMILY PRIOR TO INCIDENT:

Rented apartment in public housing	1 (64)
Rented house in public housing	2
Rented apartment in private building	3
Rented house from private owner	4
Privately owned apartment in cooperative	5
Privately owned home	6
Trailer (owned or rented)	7
Other; specify:	8
Unknown	9

24. NUMBER OF ROOMS IN LIVING QUARTERS OF SUSPECTED PERPETRATOR'S FAMILY PRIOR TO INCIDENT:

Specify number of rooms: __ __
65 66

Unknown 99

25. COST OF HOUSING (INCLUDING UTILITIES) FOR MONTH PRIOR TO INCIDENT:

Specify approximate dollar amount: __ __ __
67 68 69

Unknown 999

26. LENGTH OF TIME IN THESE ACCOMMODATIONS
PRIOR TO INCIDENT:

> Less than one year   00
> Specify approximate number of years: __ __
>   70 71
>   Unknown   99

27. DID SUSPECTED PERPETRATOR'S FAMILY REGULARLY
SHARE LIVING QUARTERS WITH OTHERS PRIOR
TO INCIDENT?

> Yes   1   (72)
> No   2
> Unknown   9

28. IN CASE WE WISH TO SEEK ADDITIONAL INFORMATION,
PLEASE SUPPLY:

Date (Schedule completed):_____

Mo. Day Yr.

Your name: _____

              First   *Middle*   *Last*

Title: _____

Agency name: _____

Address: _____

         No.   *Street*

_____

   City or Town   *County*   *State*   *Code*

Telephone and extension number: _____

THANK YOU AGAIN FOR YOUR COOPERATION

Appendix E

*Research Schedule — Circumstances
of Child Abuse*

Nationwide Epidemiologic Study of Child Abuse

26a. CIRCUMSTANCES OF CHILD ABUSE

(Insert after question #26 on p. 8 of Schedule A for the Abused Child)

Instructions: Based upon your knowledge of the incident, indicate by circling the appropriate number whether each of the following elements was "Present," "Absent," or "Unknown." Remember to supply Abused Child's I. D. No. from page No. 1 of Schedule A.

Abused Child's I. D. No. (from page #1): __ __ __ __ __ __

Element	Present	Absent	Unknown	
1. Immediate or delayed response by perpetrator to specific or suspected act(s) of child	1	2	9	(6/37)
2. Misconduct of child (by community standard) ..	1	2	9	(38)
3. Inadequately controlled anger of perpetrator ..	1	2	9	(39)
4. Resentment, rejection, etc. by perpetrator of child as person and/or of specific qualities; e.g., sex, looks, capacities, unwanted birth, illegitimacy, etc.	1	2	9	(40)
5. Repeated abuse of child by perpetrator	1	2	9	(41)
6. Persistent behavioral atypicality of child; e.g., hyperactivity, high annoyance potential, etc...	1	2	9	(42)
7. Abuse coinciding with perpetrator's sexual advances toward child	1	2	9	(43)
8. Abuse developing out of quarrel between caretakers	1	2	9	(44)
9. "Battered Child Syndrome" (involving repeated battering, multiple fractures in various stages of healing, emotional apathy regarding child's injuries, etc.)	1	2	9	(45)
10. Abuse coinciding with elements of child neglect	1	2	9	(46)
11. Marked mental and/or emotional deviation of perpetrator	1	2	9	(47)
12. Sadistic gratification of perpetrator	1	2	9	(48)
13. Alcoholic intoxication of perpetrator	1	2	9	(49)
14. Self-definition of perpetrator as stern, authoritative disciplinarian	1	2	9	(50)
15. Mounting stress on perpetrator due to life circumstances	1	2	9	(51)
16. Mother or mother substitute temporarily absent, perpetrator male	1	2	9	(52)
17. Mother or mother substitute temporarily absent, perpetrator female	1	2	9	(53)
18. Other; specify:	1	2	9	(54)

Appendix F

Testimony at Senate Hearing —
March 1973

TESTIMONY OF
DR. DAVID G. GIL, BRANDEIS UNIVERSITY*
AT HEARINGS OF
U.S. SENATE SUBCOMMITTEE ON CHILDREN AND YOUTH
ON THE "CHILD ABUSE PREVENTION ACT,"
S.1191 (93rd Congress, 1st session)
MARCH 26, 1973

Mr. Chairman, members of the Subcommittee; thank you for inviting me to testify before you. My name is David Gil. I am professor of social policy at Brandeis University in Waltham, Massachusetts.

Several years ago, at the request of the Children's Bureau of the U.S. Department of Health, Education, and Welfare, I conducted a series of nationwide studies on physical abuse of children. To my knowledge, these studies are, so far, the only systematic investigation of this phenomenon on a nationwide scale. Findings of these studies and recommendations based on these findings were published in 1970 by Harvard University Press in my book *Violence against Children.*

You have asked me specifically to focus my testimony on four issues of concern to the Subcommittee, namely, a definition of child abuse; statistics of incidence; a summary of what is known about perpetrators and victims of child abuse; and my thoughts on the legislation before you.

A Definition of Child Abuse and Neglect

Child abuse may be defined in a variety of ways, depending on the purpose for which the definition will be used. Medical practitioners engaged in the diagnosis and treatment of physically abused children tend to use definitions based on physical or anatomical symptoms identifiable in their child-patients. Mental health workers who are concerned with emotional abuse in addition to physical abuse prefer to broaden their definitions of child abuse to include signs of psychological damage. Social workers, law enforcement authorities and others whose interest

* This testimony has been edited and slightly abridged for publication here.

extends beyond the victims of abuse to perpetrators of abusive acts focus their definitions not only around observable, physical, and psychological consequences of abuse, but also around behavioral and motivational characteristics of perpetrators. Finally, legislators and social policy specialists whose concern is the protection of all children against potentially injurious acts and conditions require comprehensive definitions which take account, not only of clinical, physical, and psychological aspects of child abuse, but also of cultural, social, economic, and political factors which presumably constitute the dynamic sources of this destructive phenomenon.

Definitions, it should be noted, involve not only factual elements, but also value premises. Therefore, before suggesting a definition of child abuse which should be useful in formulating social policies for the protection and well-being of the nation's children, I wish to explicate the value premises underlying the proposed definition. These value premises may be stated as follows: Every child, despite his individual differences and uniqueness, is to be considered of equal intrinsic worth, and hence should be entitled to equal social, economic, civil, and political rights, so that he may fully realize his inherent potential, and share equally in life, liberty, and the pursuit of happiness. Obviously, these value premises are rooted in the humanistic philosophy of our Declaration of Independence. In accordance with these value premises then, any act of commission or omission by individuals, institutions, or society as a whole, and any conditions resulting from such acts or inaction, which deprive children of equal rights and liberties, and/or interfere with their optimal development, constitute, by definition, abusive or neglectful acts or conditions.

The definition proposed herewith is specific enough to identify physical and emotional abuse and neglect resulting from acts of commission or omission on the part of parents and other individual caretakers. Yet, at the same time, this definition is broad enough to cover also a wide range of abusive and damaging acts perpetrated against children by such institutions as schools, juvenile courts, and detention centers, child welfare homes and agencies, correctional facilities, and the like. Finally, this definition covers also abuse and neglect tolerated or perpetrated by society collectively. Illustrations of this latter type of abuse and neglect are malnutrition and at times starvation of expectant mothers and children, inadequate medical care of mothers, children, and whole families, substandard housing and other aspects of life in poverty-stricken neighborhoods, inadequate educational, recreational, and cultural provisions, and many more well-known conditions which tend to seriously inhibit normal and healthy human growth and development.

To round out this brief discussion of a definition of child abuse and neglect some comments seem indicated concerning the probable causes and dynamics of this complex syndrome. Many professionals, investigators, the communications media, and the general public tend to view child abuse as deviant behavior. In this view perpetrators of abuse are emotionally sick individuals and the abusive act is a symptom of their psychological disturbance. While it is probably true that numerous incidents of child abuse are indeed results of emotional illness on the part of the perpetrators, many other incidents occur in perfectly normal families. This should surprise no one as the use of physical force in the rearing and disciplining of children is widely accepted in our society. Common sense suggests that whenever corporal punishment is widely used, extreme cases will occur and children will be injured. Quite frequently acts aimed at merely disciplining children will, because of chance factors, turn into serious accidents. Our studies indicate that the widespread acceptance in our culture of physical discipline of children is the underlying factor of physical child abuse in private homes, in schools, and in various child care settings such as foster homes, detention homes, correctional institutions, and the like. It should be noted here that abusive incidents which occur in the context of emotional illness of perpetrators are also facilitated by the general cultural acceptance of the use of physical force in child rearing. For symptoms of emotional illness are often exaggerated expressions of normal traits existing in a culture. These brief comments on the causal dynamics of child abuse suggest that the real sources of this phenomenon may be deep in the fabric of society rather than within the personalities of individual perpetrators. Hence, blaming individual perpetrators, as we tend to do, means merely to shift responsibility away from society where it really belongs. The tendency to interpret social problems through individual rather than socio-cultural dynamics is, by the way, not unique in relation to child abuse. We tend to interpret most social problems as results of individual shortcomings, and we are thus able to maintain the illusion that our social system is nearly perfect and need not undergo major changes in order to overcome its many destructive societal problems.

Incidence, Distribution, and Notes on Perpetrators and Victims

Reliable information on the real incidence of child abuse is not available because of differences of opinion as to what incidents and situations are to be classified as child abuse, and also because of the non-public nature of many cases. There is some information on the number of legally reported cases. Yet, this information is of limited value since criteria and procedures for reporting vary widely across states and localities. Moreover, reported incidents are merely an unknown fraction of real incidence.

In spite of the limited validity and reliability of officially reported figures, several observations may be made on the scope and distribution of child abuse and the characteristics of perpetrators and victims. First of all, it should be noted that there is no basis to the frequently made claim that the incidence of child abuse has increased in recent years. One simply cannot talk about an increase or decrease of a phenomenon unless one has accurate counts of different periods in time. Such counts are not available, and hence, there is no basis for comparison over time. What has increased in recent decades is the awareness of, the interest in, and the concern for this phenomenon. Awareness, interest, and concern are mutually reinforcing, and hence, we end up with an impression of change in incidence. While we have no evidence for or against an increase in real levels and rates of incidence, we do have evidence of increases in reporting levels. This increase, however, seems due largely to improvements in the administration of reporting legislation and to growing awareness among physicians and others responsible for reporting.

Reporting levels are known only for 1967 and 1968, the years of the nationwide surveys. Nearly 6000 cases were reported in 1967 and over 6600 in 1968. For subsequent years figures are available only for certain states and localities. These figures suggest overall increases in reporting levels for selected jurisdictions.

Reported incidents nearly exclusively involve abuse of children in their own homes. There are hardly ever any reports on child abuse in schools and children's institutions although this kind of abuse is known to occur frequently all over the country. Public authorities seem simply reluctant to keep records of child abuse in the public domain. There are also no systematic records of the massive abuse and neglect of children due to inadequate medical care, inadequate education, and substandard living conditions as can be found in migrant labor camps, in urban and rural slums, on Indian reservations, and in many other settings. To my way of thinking, these public forms of abuse and neglect are the most serious ones in qualitative and quantitative terms, but also the least talked about, thought about, and acted upon aspects of the child abuse spectrum.

I do not want to take up your time with a recitation of statistics from the 1967 and 1968 surveys published in my book and papers. I would like to mention, however, certain unmistakable trends suggested by these statistics. While physical abuse of children is known to occur in all strata of our society, the incidence rate seems significantly higher among deprived and discriminated against segments of the population. This difference cannot be explained away by the argument that medical and other authorities are less likely to suspect and report abusive incidents among the priviledged segments of the population. For common sense supports the repeated findings of higher incidence rates among low-income and minority groups. Compared to other groups in the population, the living conditions of these deprived population segments involve much more strain and stress and frustration in daily existence which are reflected in lower levels of self-control, and in a greater propensity, to discharge angry and hostile feelings toward children. Besides, economically deprived families tend to live under more crowded conditions. Also, the rate of one parent families is much higher in these population segments, and parents have fewer opportunities to arrange substitute care for their children and take a rest from child care responsibilities. Finally, parents in economically deprived families have themselves had little exposure to educational opportunities and their child rearing methods are more traditional and rely more on physical means of discipline. We thus cannot escape the conclusion that incidence rates of child abuse on the part of individual parents tend to be higher in economically deprived families whose children are also more exposed to the many forms of societal abuse implicit in poverty.

One other widespread, erroneous impression concerning incidence rates needs to be corrected. This is the notion that child abuse affects primarily very young children. Available nationwide figures suggest that about half the reported abuse incidents involve school-aged children, and over 75 percent of reported victims of abuse were over two years old. There is also a higher rate of incidence during adolescence, especially for girls, when parents get anxious about their daughters' dating patterns. Very young children tend, however, to be more seriously injured when abused, and fatal injuries occur nearly exclusively among the very young.

Comments on S.1191

In turning now to the specific provisions of the bill before you, we must examine whether, and to what extent, its substantive provisions match its stated objectives, namely, to prevent child abuse. In my view S.1191 includes elements which could contribute to the treatment and reduction of certain types within the broad spectrum of child abuse. However, while such contributions are desirable in themselves, they seem inadequate, in terms of available knowledge, to the task of preventing all aspects of child abuse. Let me mention some of the shortcomings in the bill which should be corrected in order to strengthen it.

First of all, the language of the bill lacks a definition of child abuse and neglect. Without such a definition, it is not clear what is to be identified, treated, and prevented, nor will it be possible in the future to evaluate the effectiveness of the bill.

It would also be desirable to include in the bill a positive statement concerning the basic rights of children as persons entitled to the full protection of the U.S. Constitution and the Bill of Rights. Such a statement by the Congress could over a period of time serve as an important lever to assure these rights, if necessary, through action in the federal courts.

More specifically, it seems to me the Congress ought to outlaw through this bill all forms of physical force used against children in the public domain, in schools, and in child care facilities, under the guise of disciplining them. This form of discipline undermines the human dignity of children. It is nothing but an ancient, cruel ritual which never serves the real educational and developmental needs of children, but merely provides ventilation for the frustrations of adults. Being exposed to corporal punishment teaches children that might is right. It results in resentment and fear of their attackers. At best it achieves short-range, externally enforced, discipline based on fear, but not steady, long-term, internalized discipline based on positive identification with caring adults. We know that learning requires positive human relations which are apt to be destroyed by corporal punishment or the ever-present threat of it. It may be of interest to note that Massachusetts, where I live, is one of three states in the nation which outlawed corporal punishment in its schools and public institutions. Yet, our children and schools in Massachusetts are certainly not worse in academic achievement and overall discipline than the schools and children of other states.

One important by-product of outlawing the use of physical force in schools and institutions would be an unambiguous signal to all parents and educators that it is the sense of Congress that educators and parents should use more constructive measures to bring up and discipline children than inflicting physical pain and indignities upon them. Such a message from the Congress could initiate a rethinking of the entire child rearing context in the country. Without such rethinking and without an eventual redefinition of the status and the rights of children, child abuse can simply not be prevented.

The bill before you should also spell out what you consider a minimum living standard which the public must assure to all children in order to avoid socially sanctioned abuse and neglect. From my perspective, and in accordance with the philosophy of the Declaration of Independence, these minimum standards ought to be complete equality of rights for all children which can be achieved through systematic redistribution of our national wealth and income and of political power. You may not be ready to opt for equality right away, but in any case

207

you should specify in the bill a level of decency and adequacy of living standards below which a child would be considered abused and neglected, and hence, entitled to protection. Perhaps you could set 1976, the two-hundredth anniversary of our nation, as the target date for total equality.

I hesitate to raise questions concerning the proposed demonstration programs and the $90,000,000 to be authorized for them over the next five years. I am concerned that we may create one more illusion that child abuse can be prevented through ameliorative, clinical services. We have in the past developed many programs which were addressing the symptoms rather than the roots of social problems. I have an uncomfortable sense that the demonstration programs under this bill may fall into this category, and that at the end of five years, after spending $90,000,000, and after creating and supporting numerous service programs, nothing really significant will have happened. We must be willing to face the hard reality that preventing child abuse and neglect is possible only when we are ready to attack its sources in the fabric of our society and culture, rather than merely provide social and medical services to its victims.

I would suggest that the mandate of the proposed National Commission be broadened. In addition to studying administrative aspects of child abuse reporting, the Commission should investigate the underlying dynamics of child abuse and neglect in our society and should develop policy recommendations aimed at eliminating the sources of this ghastly phenomenon. I would also recommend that the Secretary of H.E.W. and the Director of the Office of Child Development not be ex-officio members of the Commission in order to preclude influences by officials responsible for the administration of existing policies and programs, the effectiveness of which may have to be questioned by the Commission. The Secretary and Director will have ample opportunity to comment on the findings and recommendations of the National Commission once it makes its report to the President and the Congress.

In concluding my testimony I would like to stress that my critical comments should not be interpreted as opposition to the enactment of a bill on preventing child abuse and neglect. Such a bill is certainly essential. The purpose of my critique is merely to suggest possible approaches to assure that the bill, when enacted, will accomplish the objectives implicit in its title, to prevent the abuse of our nation's children.

Mr. Chairman, members of the Subcommittee, thank you again for the opportunity to present to you my views on the protection of this nation's most important resource—our children.

Index

Abortion, availability of, 46–47, 146

Abuse: as pattern of interaction, 30; repetitions of, 113–114; data on incidents of, 118–125; typology of, 125–130

Accident, in physical abuse, 6

Adults, use of physical force between, 8, 10

Age: of abused children, 104–106, 120, 139; of parents, 109–110

Alabama, 92, 94

Alaska, 38, 92, 94

Alcoholism, 33, 128, 129, 140, 141

American Academy of Pediatrics, 38

American Humane Association: Children's Division of, 22; legislation recommended by, 23, 36, 38

American Indians, cases of child abuse among, 106

American Medical Association, on reporting of abuse, 37

Arizona, 92, 94

Arkansas, 37, 73, 92, 94

Asians, cases of child abuse among, 106

Attitudes toward child abuse, survey of, 49–70. *See also* Survey of child abuse

Automatic Interaction Detector, 53

Babysitter: female, abuse by, 129, 132, 141; male, abuse by, 130, 140

Baltimore, 103

Barton, William, 39

Battered-child syndrome: origin of term, 20, 25; related to resentment, 127, 129; relative frequency of, 138

Boardman, Helen, 20

Boise, 103

Boston, 103

Bureau of Criminal Investigation and Identification (California State Department of Justice), 84

Caffey, John, 19

California, 75, 77, 78, 93, 94; pilot study in, 81, 84–85, 126

Caretaker: defined, 7; quarrel of, as cause of abuse, 128, 129, 132, 141

Causes of child abuse, 3, 16–17, 22–23

Cheney, Kimberly B., 40–41

Chesser, Eustace, 24

Chicago, 103

Child, as cause of abuse, 29, 34

Child abuse: defined, 49–50; pro-

Index

Protective agencies, general knowledge of, 61–62
Psychological rejection, 130
Psychopathic personality, and abuse, 33
Public assistance, to families in study, 112
Publicity, and child abuse, 68
Puerto Ricans: cases of child abuse among, 106; family structure of, 108–109; severity of injuries among, 120–121
Puerto Rico, 74, 94, 96

Radio, educational programs on, 68–76
Rates of child abuse by state, 94–95; states ranked by, 99–101; absolute change in reporting of, 99, 102; linked to other factors, 99, 101
Recidivism, rate of, 140
Recommendations for prevention of child abuse, 141–148; reduction of violence in society, 141–144; reduction of poverty, 144–145; reduction of dysfunction, 145–148; family planning, 146; national health service, 146–147; child-welfare and child-protective services, 147–148
Recreational facilities, 145
Registries for reporting of child abuse: establishment of, 74–75, 90–91; classification of reports from, 92–95; not established in Texas, 96
Rejection of child, as cause of abuse, 127, 135, 140
Religion, and child abuse, 107
Reporting of child abuse, 123–124; to police, 23, 36, 123; by physicians, 37–38, 123; mandatory by law, 38; difficulties of, 39; forms for, 75–76; central registries for, 74–75, 90–91
Rhode Island, 94, 95, 98
Role reversal, in child abuse, 31

Sadism, and child abuse, 128
St. Louis, 103
Sample cohort, 102–104
Sample Unit Control and Follow-up Cards, 79
San Francisco, 103
San Mateo, 103
Schizophrenia, in abusive parents, 27, 33
Schools, reporting of child abuse by, 122, 124
Seattle, 103
Sex, of abused children, 104, 121, 139
Sexual abuse, 104, 128, 129; related to physical abuse, 6–7, 130
Sexual deviance, and abuse, 34
Silver, Larry B., 39, 41–42
Silverman, F. N., 19
Simons, Betty, 35–36
Social welfare agencies: and child abuse, 64, 66, 125; as source of help, 123
Sociocultural factors, in study of physical abuse, 12–14
South Carolina, 94, 95, 98
South Dakota, 94, 95
Staff, for survey, 87–89; study director, 87; field directors, 87–89; technical staff, 89
Standard Metropolitan Statistical Areas, 78–79, 101–102
States: differences in reporting rates among, 98–99; ranked by reporting rates, 99–101. See also individual states by name
Steele, Brandt F., 25, 30–33, 47–48
Stepfathers, as perpetrators, 117, 140
Step-parents, as perpetrators, 117
Sterilization, laws for, 46
Stress, as cause of excess force, 135, 136, 139, 140
Studies of child abuse, objectives of, 4. See also Survey (NORC); Survey of abused children
Study cohort, 102–104; nonabuse cases excluded from, 103–104

Index

Study director, for survey, 87
Subdural hematomas, 2, 19
Summit County, 103
Survey of child abuse (NORC), 49–70; method of, 50–51; issues covered by, 51–52; analysis of responses to, 52–53; characteristics of respondents to, 53–55; propensity of child abuse, 55–58; upper limit of incidence, 58–60; general knowledge of, 60–61; knowledge of protective agencies, 61–62; reactions to, 62–64; treatment of child and perpetrators, 65–67; knowledge of educational programs, 67–68; summary of, 69–70
Survey of abused children reported legally, 71–132; study procedures, 73–74; central registries, 74–75, 90–91; report forms for, 75–76; case screening, 76–77; follow-up procedures for, 77–78; comprehensive study for, 78–81; research schedules, 81–83; reporting of fatalities, 83–84; pilot study for, 84–85, 87; analysis of findings of, 85–86; costs and resources, 86–89; utilization of, 89–91; findings of, 92–132

Television, educational programs on, 67–68
Tennessee, 94, 95
Texas, 38, 74, 75, 77, 78, 94, 95; no central registry in, 96; rates of reporting in, 98
Tolerance toward child abuse, 58, 65, 69
Trauma, associated with skeletal lesions, 19

Typology of child abuse, 125–130, 140; factor analysis of, 130–132

Unemployment, and child abuse, 34
United States, rates for reporting of child abuse in, 98–99
U. S. Children's Bureau, 3; bibliography by, 18; conference called by (1962), 21; guidelines by, 36, 38; legislation urged by, 72
Utah, 94, 95

Vermont, 94, 95
Violence against children: related to general adult violence, 14, 142; collective, 15
Virgin Islands, 94, 96
Virginia, 94, 95, 98

Washington, D.C., 72, 79, 93, 94, 96
Washington (state), 38
West Virginia, 94, 95
Westchester County, 103
Whites: percentages of child abuse among, 106; family structure of, 108–109; severity of injuries of, 120–121. See also Nonwhites
Wisconsin, 77, 78, 94, 95; increased reports from, 98
Woolley, P. V., 19
Worcester County, 103
Wyoming, 94, 95

Young, Leontine, 24

Zalba, Serapio R., 25

216

6.95